BY

REV. J. T. CRANE, D. D.,

Of the Newark Conference.

WITH AN INTRODUCTION,

BY

BISHOP E. S. JANES.

"*For the Commandment is a Lamp; and the Light is Life; and Reproofs of Instruction are the Way of Life.*" PROVERBS VI, 23.

CINCINNATI:
HITCHCOCK AND WALDEN.

NEW YORK:
CARLTON AND LANAHAN.
1870.

CONTENTS.

CHAPTER II.

TRUE RECREATION.

CHAPTER III.

THE THEATER.

CHAPTER IV.

HORSE-RACING.

CHAPTER V.

BASE BALL.

CHAPTER VI.

DANCING.

CHAPTER VII.

CARDS, CHESS, AND BILLIARDS.

CHAPTER VIII.

NOVELS AND NOVEL-READING.

CHAPTER IX.

SOCIAL GATHERINGS.

CHAPTER X.

APPEAL TO THE YOUNG MEMBERS OF THE CHURCH.

CHAPTER XI.

APPEAL TO THE CHURCH.

INTRODUCTION.

THE subject of which this book treats—"Popular Amusements"—is one of grave interest to the Church and to society in general. The Discipline of the Methodist Episcopal Church has always required its members and probationers, as an evidence of religious earnestness, to refrain from "such diversions as can not be used in the name of the Lord Jesus," and also from "singing those songs or reading those books which do not tend to the knowledge or love of God." In the following passages of Holy Scripture, worldly amusements or pleasures are denounced by God: "He that loveth pleasure shall be a poor man." "Therefore hear now this, thou that art given to pleasure, that dwellest carelessly." The consequences referred to in this quotation are stated in the following verses of the chapter. Being "lovers of pleasure more than lovers of God," is classed by Timothy as one of the worst attributes of wicked men. How terrible is this statement: "But she that liveth in pleasure is dead while she liveth!" Consider, also, this Scripture precept: "And whatsoever ye do in word or deed, do all in the name of the Lord Jesus." In view of these and like Scripture utterances, how is it possible to believe that exciting, dissipating, worldly amusements are compatible with spiritual life or devotional enjoyment?

The experience of multitudes corresponds with these teachings of the Discipline and the Bible. Take this instance. On one occasion Mr. Charles Wesley was warning the people against so-called "harmless diversions," and declared that by them he had been kept dead to God, asleep in the arms of Satan, and secure in a state of damnation for eighteen years. There were three ministers present besides Mr. Wesley. Mr. Meriton cried out,

"And I for twenty-five!" "And I," exclaimed Mr. Thompson, "for thirty-five!" "And I," added Mr. Bennett, "for about seventy!" These cases of Christian ministers suggest how general and how baleful is the influence of these diversions.

This evil, perhaps, is not peculiar to any clime or age. Diversions, indeed, change with the times. The fashionable follies of the last century are now deemed matters of wonder and derision, just as the follies of our day may be laughed at a hundred years hence. But worldliness, fashion, and frivolity are always at work inventing questionable pleasures and ingenious arguments for their defense. Possibly it is unreasonable to expect but one opinion as to what is allowable in the way of recreation. As there are various degrees of knowledge and piety in the Church, and various degrees of conscientiousness among even those who do not profess religion, there will be conflicting opinions on the subject, one condemning what another defends, and each wondering at the scrupulousness or the laxity of his neighbor. On this, as on all other subjects, Christians should judge each other charitably, but by the Scripture standard.

This little volume takes what I believe to be the true ground in regard to the diversions discussed in it—the only ground which is defensible in theory and safe in practice. The Methodist Episcopal Church is strong in numbers, in wealth, and in social position. If we maintain the strict morals and the deep spirituality—and they go together—which have hitherto been our aim, we shall be in the years to come, in the hands of God, an instrumentality of unlimited power for good. If, on the other hand, we become weak in our belief and lax in discipline, the members of the Church fashionable and frivolous, and the ministers doubtful and indefinite in doctrine, and feeble in utterance, we shall lose the position we have held among the Churches of the Lord Jesus Christ, and God will raise up another people to take our place and our crown. But we trust in God we shall never, as a Church, be moved from our old foundation in doctrines or in morals. Though worldliness and unbelief may continue to assail her, yet the Church is strong in that power which overcomes the world.

Recently the advocates of popular amusements have been both bold and insidious. They have used the pulpit, the press, and so-called "Christian Associations" to propagate their views. In some cases they recommend what are considered the less objectionable diversions to prevent indulgence in the more objectionable ones—on the principle "of two evils choose the less." But in morals the lesser evil always tends to introduce the greater. The proposition, therefore, is a most mischievous one. To those individuals among us who have been disturbed in their religious convictions on this question, by the deceptive pleas of those who defend or advocate worldly amusements, this book will be found an effective helper. In it Dr. Crane speaks the sentiments of the Methodist Church. We believe the position we have hitherto held on this subject is Scriptural and safe, and that, rigid as the world deems it, our disciplinary rule is wise and needful.

These fashionable diversions are not necessary

for the health of the body or mind, but are harmful to both. All the recreation that any pious, sensible person needs is provided in the variety of his duties, and the many and ample sources of rational enjoyment. Does the studious, hard-working minister need recreation? Let him find it in turning from the severe study of theology to biography, or poetry, or rhetoric, or logic? Does he need a still greater change? Let him take up for the time being astronomy, or geology, or history. Does he need physical as well as mental relaxation and change? Certainly he can find them in his pastoral work—in visiting the sick, in instructing childhood, in looking after the general interests of the Church, in walking, or riding, or attending to the interests of his family, or enjoying their society. Surely, here is a vast realm in which he can find rest and recreation both for soul and body, and grow wiser and better all the while. Does the layman of the Church need recreation as a relief from the monotonou and exhausting labors and cares that come upon him daily? Let him find it in gardening, in cultivating flowers, in reading, in music, in Christian activities, in domestic offices and intercourse, in social visiting, in attending instructive lectures, in attending devotional meetings. These are rational, spiritual, satisfying enjoyments. None but the weak, who think more of conformity to the world than of conformity to Christ, hanker after any other.

Dr. Crane has treated this subject clearly, Methodistically, and Scripturally. The book is a timely and useful addition to the literature of the Church. I trust the publishers will put it in an attractive form, and that it will have an extensive circulation, do good to many souls, and bring much glory to God.

E. S. JANES.

NEW YORK, *June* 24, 1869.

Popular Amusements.

CHAPTER I.

RECREATION A GOOD THING.

"*And the streets of the city shall be full of boys and girls, playing in the streets thereof.*" Zech. viii, 5.

THE prophet thus, as with a single stroke of his pencil, paints a beautiful picture of peace, plenty, and public security. In times of riot and wild disorder, the children are kept within doors, that they may be out of the way of harm. In time of war, children may be seen in the streets of the city; but they are there clinging in terror to the hands of their parents, and surrounded by the confusion and alarm of a population flying from the foe. When famine reigns, a few children may be found in the streets; but they are the wan, emaciated victims of hunger, who wander from their desolate homes to beg, with tears and outstretched hands, for bread. If the war or the famine continue its ravages, the number of children steadily decreases. In seasons of public calamity, little children die, as the tender blossoms of Spring perish beneath the volleys of untimely hail. In the prophetic picture, therefore, the numbers of the children, their merry sports, and the public places where they are playing, all give token of the safety and prosperity of a people whom the Lord protects and blesses.

But if this be so, it can not be wrong for boys and girls to play. A doubt upon this point would mar the representation and destroy the force of the imagery. No, let the children play—not, indeed, without limit; not to the neglect of study, nor of such useful labor as they ought to perform; not in modes that transgress Divine law, nor in the company of those who will teach them corrupt language and evil deeds: still, let the children play. Let them leap, and laugh, and shout. Let them have their playthings and their pets. Let them not fear the sun nor the winds of heaven, though their cheeks ripen like peaches in the light and the heat, and though faces and garments occasionally show that man still retains an affinity for the dust whence he was originally taken.

Let the youth have their seasons of recreation. Their amusements, indeed, ought to be of a higher intellectual type than those of little children. Nevertheless, amusements are still lawful and expedient. Let there be times when the student shall lay aside the book, and the clerk, the apprentice, and the farmer's boys and girls forget their work. Let the youth, rich or poor, humble or exalted, at home beneath the parental roof, or in the employ or under the care of strangers, have their periods of rest and recreation. And if the time and the mode are wisely chosen, there will be no loss but a real gain to all concerned. The student will return to the lesson with a better courage and a clearer brain, and the fingers which are busy with the affairs of the house, the office, the shop, or the field will ply their task more nimbly.

Let middle life, too, immersed, as it is, in the cares and toils of this busy existence, have its hours of leisure and freedom. Brain and muscle both need rest, and the burden will feel the lighter for being occasionally laid aside. Industry is indeed a virtue. Let every man, woman, and child have something useful to do, and do it. I would not, for one moment even, seem to defend idleness, or apologize for the follies of the aimless devotee of shallow pleasures; yet I am persuaded that not a few of our most valued workers in fields of lofty usefulness would find their heads growing gray less rapidly if they could be induced to take an occasional rest.

And let the aged, also, have their recreations. It is not unbecoming for them to devote an hour, now and then, to the quiet pleasures which smooth the brow and wreathe the lip with smiles. In itself it is just as pious to laugh as to weep, and there are a great many cases where it is wiser and better to laugh. For the old and the young there are social enjoyments and recreations which brighten the passing moments and leave no shadow behind them; which send us back to the graver employments of life with a lighter heart and stronger frame. Travelers sometimes tell us that of all the nations of the earth the Americans have the fewest public holidays. This, if true, is not much to be regretted. A public holiday is very apt to be a public nuisance, disturbing the peace of quiet people, and multiplying temptations for the young and the thoughtless. If there are anniversaries and days of patriotic uproar, to which gunpowder and alcohol alone can do justice, it must be confessed that the multiplication of them is not desirable. Moreover, if custom fails to prescribe times and modes of recreation, it leaves families and societies the freer to choose for themselves.

But on what principle are we to choose our recreations? Are we at liberty to follow the multitude, inquiring, not for the best reason, but the latest fashion? No intelligent Christian will fail to see that he must be as conscientious in his play as in his work. Ever applicable, ever authoritative, the divine deposition of the unchanging principles of justice, safety, and right, the holy law is designed for all hours of the individual life, even as it is designed for all ages of the world.

The question of amusements for religious people is one of the great problems of the day. The very successes of the Gospel in our own land have brought upon the Church perils which were unknown in the ages when the victories of the truth were less decisive In the Apostolic age, when the world was heathen, and God's people a little flock in the midst of their enemies, every man and woman was either Christian or pagan, one thing or the other; the Church and the world were separated by a chasm wide and deep, and the only feelings common to both parties were distrust and aversion. Again: not very many years ago, in our own community, there were few young people to be found among the members of the various Churches. The gay multitude pursued their pleasures with a reckless extravagance and a giddy disregard of the realities of life which alarmed the soberminded, and effectually repelled the conscientious. The Church marched in order of battle, all eyes looking for the foe, and all weapons bared for conflict. The world, not always in the humor for direct attack, went on its own way, strong in the fancied strength of numbers, and sometimes tried to laugh, and sometimes affected to sneer at the scruples of the pious. Each was a compact force, openly wearing its own uniform and arraying itself under its own banner. The antagonism was universally recognized and felt.

But in our own times, and in most sections of our land, the truth has conquered. The world no longer carries on a fierce and open war against the religion of the Bible. The Church possesses so much worth, intelligence, wealth, and social power, that the worldly part of the community feel that it would not be wise for them to try to keep aloof from the pious and set up for themselves. On the contrary, the world deems it policy to nestle close up to the Church, and in many cases it conducts itself so respectably, and is so correct in outward seeming, that it takes a sharp eye to distinguish the one from the other. Not setting itself in array against the truth, but rather avowing a sort of theoretic belief of it, the world, after all, is unchanged. Its eyes are blind, its heart is hard, and its aims and motives are "of the earth earthy." It wishes to walk by the side of the Church, and hand in hand with it, but with steady pressure it draws in the direction of lax morality. Not having received the heavenly anointing, it fails to see how "exceeding broad" the Divine Law is. It is constantly pleading for a larger license, a wider range of sensuous enjoyments than is consistent with the true piety which transforms and saves. Thus it clings to the Church, arguing, inviting, urging; and wherever to its own dull vision the path ceases to be clear, it sweeps off swiftly and invariably into the realms of darkness and danger.

And the Church, too, is not in haste to separate itself wholly from the large class found just outside the line of strict religious profession. We admire their intelligence and amiability; their many worthy traits of character and conduct. Their companionship is pleasant, and we would like to retain it, and, therefore, we are strongly tempted, for the sake of it, to make concessions on the various moral questions in debate between us and them. Another influence is silently and yet powerfully at work. Unless we consent that they shall marry in the Chinese style—without having previously exchanged a word or even seen each other's faces—our young people must have opportunities to get acquainted and form attachments. In making their selections they like to take a wide range of observation. A deal of skirmishing generally precedes the final conquest. The young Church-member does not feel inclined to refuse the acquaintance of moral, intelligent, agreeable young people simply on the ground that they are not professors of religion. The young people of the world see that if they do not keep near the Church they cut themselves off from the best portions of society. Without violence no rigid lines of social separation can be drawn between the Church and the general community. The two parties hold to each other, each inviting, pleading, trying to draw the other in its own direction, in the path of its own principles and tendencies. The one is ready to yield all that can be conceded without an abandonment of truth and duty; the other, like Herod under the influence of John's preaching, fears, and listens, and does "many things."

Nor is it clear that utter separation is desirable. We can be instrumental in saving only those who are within our reach. How shall we bring others within the range of our influence, and at the same time keep wholly beyond the range of theirs? How shall we lift up others and yet not feel their weight? If we drive from us all who have failed thus far to come up to our standard, we lessen the area of our usefulness—we throw away precious opportunities to do good. The

Church, if faithful, is not imperiled by this antagonism of moral forces. It must show itself the more powerful of the two, and "overcome the world." Surely, if truth is strong, if fixed principles of action furnish a solid fulcrum on which to place our levers, we ought to move the world, and not the world us.

It follows, therefore, that if the young members of the Church, and the young people just outside the line of religious profession, are to unite in social gatherings and recreations, duty demands that we stand firm, while courtesy and reason, to say nothing of still higher motives, require that others yield. No labored argument is needed to show this. The lover of frivolous pleasures can not plead that religious convictions impel him to his follies. When youthful Christians fear and resist, saying, "Conscience forbids," he can not reply, "*My* conscience commands." When the Christian remonstrates, saying, "To do this might imperil my soul," the other can not answer, "*Not* to do it would imperil mine." The worldly can only plead that they see no evil where others see it, and that they are ready to venture where others fear to go. Thus they virtually confess that they are dull in vision and hard in heart.

And so we can not come down to the level to which they would invite us. If they desire us to meet on common ground, we must be permitted to select the place. If we yield to them, we sacrifice our principles and our peace. If they yield to us, they lose, at the utmost, only a little temporary pleasure. Let the worldly and the gay, therefore, say no more about our Puritanic notions. They see, and ought to confess, that almost of necessity they tend to place the standard of morals too low, and that when the Church and the world differ in regard to what is allowable and right, there are a thousand chances to one that the Church is right and the world is wrong. If the religion of Christ laid no restrictions on us which the trifling mind and the unrenewed heart felt to be unwelcome, or even burdensome, we might well suspect that it was the invention of men.

CHAPTER II.

TRUE RECREATION.

"*And let them measure the pattern.*" Ezekiel xliii, 10.

WHAT amusements, then, are rational and allowable? and to what extent may we indulge in them? We desire, before we discuss specific modes of recreation, to lay down certain general principles, and indicate what we believe to be the true method of reasoning on the subject, so that the reader, keeping these in mind, will see why we approve or condemn hereafter, even when, for the sake of brevity, the conclusion is given in few words.

First of all, then, we inquire, What is the true design of recreation? The mere pleasure of the hour is certainly not the sole object at which we should aim, regardless of all other considerations. A degree of enjoyment may be desirable; and yet the temporary pleasure is not all. The true idea of rational recreation is expressed in the very name. The aim is to renew, restore, create again. It is to lay aside the more serious avocations of life for a brief space, that we may resume them with new vigor. It is to make a little truce with toil and care, that we may return to the battle with stouter hearts and keener weapons. We rest, that we may be the better prepared for work. Rational recreation never loses sight of duty. It teaches us to seek, now and then, a little leisure, that we may be able to labor the harder and the longer; to be gay and merry, only that we may be the more susceptible, in its time, of all solemn, holy emotion. Recreation, in the true sense of the term, is not only free from evil, but it is full of good intents, aiming, above all, to aid us in the great concerns which look beyond the horizon of the present life. We shake off care, but not conscience. We do not lay aside the service of God and take a day to ourselves, but strive to win the benediction pronounced upon "the man that feareth always."

To make the discussion as practical as possible, we name eight different points of view from which we may consider any diversion proposed to us:

1. *Our recreations should be innocent in themselves.*

Compared with eternal interests, present enjoyment is as dust in the balance. However exhilarating or beneficial to health the advocates of any amusement may claim that their favorite diversion is, if there be an element of wrong in it, it must be condemned without hesitation or reserve. If it involves any transgression of Divine law; if it leads us to disregard the welfare of our fellow; if the pleasure is purchased by pain wantonly inflicted upon man, or beast, or bird, or insect; if it tends to render us frivolous or reckless, or in any way leaves us farther from God and heaven, less conscientious, less devotional, less tender in heart, less active and earnest in all good works, we must condemn it, no matter how fascinating it may be, no matter what may be the numbers or the social position of those who favor it. Of all the poor excuses for sin, one of the poorest and meanest is the plea that we trampled on the law of God and defied his justice for the sake of amusement.

2. *Our recreations must never be suffered to lessen our influence as followers of Christ.*

A good name is an element of strength. Unless those around us have confidence in our sincerity, we are shorn of our moral power. No matter how clear our integrity may be in our own eyes, if we fail to convince the world of it; if we seem to be less careful of obligation, less mindful of the right than Christians should be, there will be a cloud of distrust hovering about us wherever we are, and we will find ourselves shut out of some of the noblest fields of effort. The world watches our recreations as well as our more weighty employments. We need not, indeed, be governed always by the reproaches of the censorious and the complaints of the morose; still, it is never safe to be indifferent to popular opinion. Even where we discover no evident wrong, we should not, for the sake of mere momentary pleasure, give ourselves to any pursuit which bears a suspicious name or is surrounded by doubtful associations. Even in Christian communities public opinion does not tend to be fanatically rigid, and we may be sure that what it condemns we will find it safe to avoid.

Nor should our recreations ever be of such a character as to wound our fellow-Christians. It is true, you need not always be controlled by the views of this or that member of the Church, who, perhaps, does not abound in the intelligence and wisdom which give weight to opinion. But what does your pastor think? If you and he differ, who is probably right? Look about you. See who they are in your community who are universally acknowledged as the real disciples of Christ, by whose aggregate good name the Church stands in reputation. What do they think? Where they doubt, you may well hesitate. Even if they should seem needlessly scrupulous, you may be sure of one thing—you will not find it dangerous to follow their counsel.

And you have no right to treat their admonitions with indifference. You can not, without peril, go counter to their views of duty. Whatever may be the abstract right or wrong of the thing in question, this evil effect, at least, will follow your rejection of their advice: you will separate yourselves from your pious exemplars and guides; the chasm, however narrow at first, will widen with time; the society of your fellow-Christians will lose its charm; the social forces which helped, more than you are aware of, to hold you to your duty, will lose their power; the Tempter will excite in your heart now anger at others, now doubts of yourself, and the process, unless arrested, will end in spiritual wreck and ruin.

3. *Our recreations should never be so chosen or so pursued as to interfere with the full and faithful performance of the sober duties of life.*

Childhood and youth are not, as some fancy, a period of mere waiting, a sort of play spell before school begins. In regard to the success of after life, it is the hour of precious opportunities which come but once. It is the foundation upon which the whole future edifice is to rest.

If a child should never learn the things which an infant one year old usually knows, he would grow up in a state of idiocy. In their very plays, as we term them, children investigate the properties of matter, acquire ease and skill in managing the bones and muscles of their own frames, and learn the contents of the great world, which is all so new to them. Youth has its work, and all after excellence is connected with the industry and care with which that work is done. The mind is to be cultured, the reason exercised, the fancy curbed, the memory stored with treasure, the whole intellect disciplined and prepared for continuous, patient labor. In youth the avocation is to be chosen, the great problems of time and eternity revolved, and the solemn journey begun. He that would be wise must not dream away the golden hours in empty visions of what he would like to be, but rouse himself and prepare to encounter soberly the great duties before him. He has not a moment to lose. He must look and listen, read and remember;

he must reflect, and reason, and judge; he must will and do wisely and well, and every day gather strength for other days to come.

If, therefore, diversions are of such a nature, or are so pursued as to induce an idle, dreamy, inconstant frame of mind, making it an annoyance and a burden to be summoned to real work in careful thinking or patient doing, a resolute grapple with the plain responsibilities of ordinary life, something is wrong. When the imagination has outgrown the judgment, and the mind revolts at reality and delights to dwell in the realms of fancy, building destinies out of airy nothing, we can see foreshadowed, as we look into the future, only bitter disappointment and failure.

4. *Our recreations must promote health.*

Health is the material of which efficient life is made. They who squander it cut short the day which God assigned them, cloud it with weakness and pain, and lessen the practical results of living. To do this willfully, deliberately, in the chase after mere pleasu is not a small sin. Our Creator requires of us the wise and faithful use of the various elements of activity and power with which he has endowed us. If, then, the hours spent in what we call diversion be followed by exhaustion; if the evening of mirth be succeeded by a day in which the brow is clouded, the frame languid, the mind irritable, the whole being disordered, there has been something wrong, either in the nature of the amusement or the manner in which it was pursued. To be well and strong, if we may, is our duty. Our recreations should not lessen but increase our power to will and to do. They are designed to sharpen the tools with which we work, and if the process which we adopt mars the blade our methods are bad. The value of the mode is to be estimated not merely by the present pleasure, but by the power gained by it. If the mower in the meadow is enchanted with the rattling, ringing music which accompanies the whetting of the scythe, but at each repetition finds the edge duller than before, till finally he can not cut the grass at all, he might as well be standing among those whom "no man hath hired."

5. *Our recreations should not be unduly expensive.*

Money is power. It may be made to feed the hungry and clothe the naked. It may be employed in teaching the ignorant and reclaiming those that wander. It plays an important part in all good works. He that squanders money throws away the ability to do good. He "wastes his Lord's substance." In Christ's description of the day of Judgment, the stress is laid, not upon names, professions, and beliefs, but the tangible fruits of piety. We must beware, therefore, lest our self-indulgences tax our purse too heavily, and leave too little for good deeds. The hour is not far distant when the memory of one kind act will be to us the source of more pleasure than the recollection of all the selfish joys of a life-time. It is to be feared that some professors of religion, who lack neither opportunities nor means to do much, will make rather a poor showing at the last great day.

6. *Recreation should never lose sight of the value of time.*

Time is one of God's most precious gifts. It is the material of which life is made, the field in which eternal destinies germinate, the Summer in which divine things grow. We have no more right to lay plans to "kill time" than to kill ourselves. The suicide rebels against the duties assigned him by Providence, deserts his post, and throws from him the years otherwise allotted him. The aimless, idle soul, without a purpose or a plan, whom no incentive can stir, and to whom lif is a weariness, because there seems nothing for which to live, commits a daily suicide. Wealth is no excuse for uselessness. When children play all their lives because their fathers worked hard from youth to old age, they take rather a doubtful way to honor their parents. If a man has no sober aim in life, no worthy object for which he is striving, God will not hold him guiltless. Genuine recreation harmonizes with all high and holy enterprise. It does not make us drones, living upon the stores which the working bees of the hive have accumulated, but teaches us, like the son of Saul, weary and faint in the rapid pursuit of the foes of Israel, to stop for a moment to taste the honey dripping in the forest, that our "eyes may brighten," and we press on with swifter feet. Genuine recreation wastes no time, but, on the contrary, treasures up the golden moments with a miser's care. Diversions indulged in beyond measure cease, therefore, to be recreations, and become a criminal waste of God's precious gift.

7. *Our recreations ought to improve the mind.*

They should not, indeed, burden the mental powers; nevertheless, they ought not to be childish and without meaning. There should always be enough of thought involved to keep the mind pleasantly and not unprofitably occupied. For this reason recreation is best pursued not alone, but socially. Cheerful, intelligent conversation is itself one of the best of recreations. The heart is improved, the mind is roused into new vigor and fruitfulness, the thoughts are wrested away from toil and care, and smiles break through the gloom like sunshine bursting through the rifted clouds.

8. *Our recreations should be productive of genuine enjoyment.*

The very idea of recreation includes that of pleasure. If it leaves us sad or dull it fails of its true aim. It ought to make the eye bright and the cheek glow. It should have an affinity for smiles, and pleasant words, and mirthful thoughts which glance like the play of the northern Aurora when the night is cloudless. It should leave memories in which there is no tinge of shame or regret. We attach importance to the innocent pleasure of the moment, because the benefit is derived in no small degree from the mind's release from its burdens. A company of school-girls, silent and prim, taking their daily march with the mechanical accuracy of soldiers, lose half the value of the air and exercise. The merchant gains little who goes on a solitary fishing excursion, and sits gazing at vacancy, with his brain full of invoices and sales, units and tens, while the fish run away with his line. Let the young and the old seek suitable recreation and enjoy it, in a genial, happy, mirthful spirit. Innocent mirth is neither unchristian nor undignified. If a man can not laugh, there is something the matter with him. Either his morals or his liver is disordered. He needs either repentance or pills. Some of earth's greatest and purest men have been noted for their mirthful tendencies. Socrates often amused himself in play with children. Luther loved dogs, and birds, and wit, and laughter, and by his rousing peals kept his lungs in good order for his theological wars. Thomas Walsh, one of the best, but not the most hilarious of men, complained that John Wesley's wit and humor made him laugh more than his conscience approved; but Mr. Walsh died in his youth, while Mr. Wesley filled up the measure of eighty-eight busy, happy years.

These are some of the principles which underlie the subject before us. It now remains to apply these principles to specific plans and methods of recreation. In the scales thus constructed let us proceed to weigh the various diversions and amusements which claim our suffrages. We will look first at the more public and pretentious of these candidates for our approval.

CHAPTER III.

THE THEATER.

"Can a man take fire in his bosom and his clothes not be burned?" Prov. vii, 27.

THE theater has its apologists and advocates. It is said to be a good place to learn history, human nature, and all that. Some plays are declared to be "as good as a sermon." Assuming this to be true, it might not be out of place to inquire how often these good plays are performed, and how they "draw." What proportion does this good sort bear to the general mass of plays nightly set before the public? Questions multiply as we consider the subject. If plays are as good as sermons, how happens it that, as a rule, those who admire plays have no love for sermons? Moreover, if the theater is a preacher of righteousness, or essays to be such, where are the "gifts, grace, and usefulness" which are the evidences of its call to the good work? There may be no special lack of a certain kind of gifts, but where is the grace? Does it adorn the character and conduct of the performers? Unless these as a class have been grievously slandered for two thousand years, we must look elsewhere. And where is the proof of moral and religious usefulness? It has no existence. The fact is, to plead for the theater on the ground that its moral influence is good, is to act a bigger farce than was ever put upon the stage. When a young man, who has been religiously trained, begins to frequent the theater, quiet observers see that he has taken the first step of a downward course; and if connected with him in business relations, or otherwise, they govern themselves accordingly. When a young man, whose reputation has suffered by his wild and reckless conduct, ceases to attend the play and begins to attend Church, his true friends begin to have hope in regard to him. All who have in any degree looked into the matter, know that the disreputable and the vile shun the Church, and crowd to the theater, while many who are plying foul trades depend upon the play-house, not only to bring the victim within their reach, but to undermine his virtue, lull his caution to sleep, and prepare him to fall in the net spread for him. Build a theater where you will, and straightway drinking saloons, gambling dens, and brothels spring up all about it and flourish under its shadow. All manner of vice, and villainy, and shame grows green and rank in the polluted soil which it creates.

Some years ago, the owners of a certain theater in one of our great cities, resolving to conduct it in a "respectable" way, attempted to shut out, as far as practicable, all whose vocation was infamous. This they thought would be easily effected by refusing admittance to every "lady not accompanied by a gentleman." This simple measure accomplished all that was expected of it, and a great deal more. The class aimed at were indeed excluded; but, alas for the proprietors! the consequent loss of patronage was so great that the establishment no longer paid current expenses, and the owners found themselves compelled either to close their doors altogether or open them to the cattle that herd in the upper galleries. The fact is plain to all who are willing to see, that the theater thrives by the vice and crime of the community. It is a buzzard that lives on carrion. To succeed it must be content to be the hunting-ground where infamy shall snare its victims, and lead them "as an ox to the slaughter." More than this, the performances and the whole arrangement must be adapted to the low moral level of an audience gathered up from the particular quarters where alone patrons can be found in sufficient numbers to make the play-house a paying institution. A successful theater must be on good terms with the grogshop and the brothel.

The whole thing is one of strategy and calculation. As the skillful angler puts on his hooks the bait at which the fish will bite most eagerly—no matter what it is, worm or bug, or artificial fly—so the crafty manager of a theater surveys society, and considers what plays, what style of acting, what style of dress among the actors and actresses will most surely attract the crowd. He is aware that the really religious portion of the community regard the Church and the theater as antagonists, and look upon him as one who is laboring to undo all that they are trying to accomplish. He knows that many people of culture and high social position regard his profession as dishonorable and degrading. These classes he leaves out of his calculation, because they are beyond his reach. But a great multitude remain, composed, in part, of the young and the heedless, fond of noise, and show, and excitement, and in part of the corrupt and the vile, the hungry beasts and birds of prey, who want victims. Among these he must find his patrons and his profits. In aiming to gather them into his fold, he must gratify their peculiar taste. He knows that he can please them only by keeping them well pleased with themselves. Will he do this by means of plays which, from the first line to the last, brand vice as infamous, and exalt virtue and honor? He knows his calling better. The people who compose his audiences do not come to the theater to be made ashamed of themselves. They would not listen to such a play, but would go out of the house, in the midst of the performances, angrily muttering that when they want a sermon they will go to the Church for it. The manager must set forth more savory viands. He must address himself to empty minds and cater to animal passions. He that undertakes to feed a flock of crows need not provide either the manna of the Scripture or the nectar and ambrosia of which classic fable tells.

As the calculations of an almanac are made for the particular latitude where it is expected to sell, so all the arrangements and appliances of the theater are carefully adapted to those classes of society which are low both in intelligence and in morals. Tragedy, to be popular, must not only deal in crime, but in loathsome, nauseous crime. Popular comedy must ridicule religion, and show how much better acute and crafty villainy is than simple truth and innocence. Immodesty is one of the attractions relied upon to draw the brutal herd. The female performers on the stage must expose their persons in a style which would be branded as grossly indecent anywhere else. Let a fact be stated in illustration. One of the high officers of the municipal government of London recently issued a circular, addressed to the proprietors and managers of the various theaters, remonstrating against the indecent costumes of the stage, and urging reform. What the effect of the appeal was upon the parties addressed does not appear; but an actress replied, in one of the public journals, declaring that she is aware of all that the circular asserts, but affirming that she and all the female performers are powerless in the case, the managers demanding the immodest costume as one of the necessities of the drama.

It is not probable that the British stage is more corrupting and immoral than the American. There is not a city on the face of the globe where the theater can live unless it goes down into depths of infamy, and becomes the panderer of all vice and shame. It is true that a few, whom the world calls moral and respectable, are sometimes found at the play-house, but they are so few that play-writers and stage managers, having an eye to the financial receipts and successes, look in other directions, and graduate the plot, and the sentiments, and the scenes, and, above all, the costume of the performers, for a lower moral level. Not seldom is the play itself a weak, unmeaning thing, which is intended to serve merely as a pretext for the shameless exhibitions deemed necessary in order to fill the house.

The theater will never be reformed. The truly refined despise it, the wise and the good abhor it. It must find its support among the thoughtless, the ignorant, and the vicious. It must be indecent or die.

And so it comes to this: immodesty is a part of the stock in trade of the play-house. There must be indecent exposure, else the foul crew that frequent the theater, and upon whose patronage it lives, will care nothing for its performances. In vain is the genius of poets and authors! In vain are all the tinsel glories of the show! Even the play which is "as good as a sermon" will be a failure, and its lofty periods be declaimed to an empty house, unless modesty and honor are sacrificed to gratify the lowest passions of the most debased of human kind. Where did any evil invention of man ever bear upon its front the stamp of infamy in plainer, deeper lines?

Why, then, should those who believe in virtue sustain, or help to sustain, that which can not exist at all except in alliance with vice and shame? How can those who believe in God and love his cause aid this engine of the devil? Do they know how valuable their help is, and at what a price the engineers are willing to purchase even their silence? When the infamous classes of society find themselves the only occupants of the theater, they will be apt to abandon it. It will not then serve their purpose. Rats can not live in an empty barn. Thieves can not live by robbing each other. The seller of alcohol can not prosper long by selling to the same set of customers. As soon as the drunkard has lost all, his very presence becomes hateful to the man who has ruined him. A whisky-shop resembles a college, in that it needs a class of freshmen to replace every class that graduate. And so with all forms of vice; they need a constant supply of new victims. When one set of unfortunates have been picked to the bone others must be had.

And thus the theater is a valuable auxiliary to certain characters, seeing that it brings their prey within their reach. How, then, can a Christian hesitate one moment in regard to duty? By what blindness, by what mode of self-delusion, can virtuous women be induced to patronize an institution which lives on the ruins of virtue? How can they sit among the spectators, and look upon wanton exhibitions and shameless exposures of person, such as would anywhere else crimson every modest cheek with shame or redden it with the consciousness of insult? How can they sit among the crowd, while eager eyes are looking down wolfishly upon the brother, the lover, or the husband who sits by their side, and foul hearts are wondering whether he ever comes to this place alone, and whether he is beyond the reach of their subtile arts? How can virtuous women consent ever to set foot within the walls of a theater, when they know that the very air is thick with infamy and death, and when every one who sees them there knows that they know it?

There is an old story to this effect: An angel, flying on some errand of mercy, met Satan, who was dragging away a monk, clad in full canonicals. The angel stopped the adversary, and demanded the release of the prisoner, saying that his very robes showed that he was a holy man, to whom Satan could have no claim. "But he is mine," was the emphatic reply. "I found him on my premises; I caught him at the theater!"

Even heathen moralists and philosophers have condemned the stage as tending to corrupt public morals. This was the ground taken by Plato, Seneca, and Cicero, two thousand years ago. The early Christian writers, the fathers of the Church, denounced the theater. It is safe to say that the piety and intelligence of the Church have always condemned it. John Wesley, the founder of our Church, gave his judgment in no equivocal terms: "The present stage entertainments not only sap the foundation of all religion, but tend to drinking and debauchery of every kind, which are constant attendants on these entertainments."

Truly, the play-house is no place for a follower of Christ. Like the Babylon of the Revelator, it is "*the hold of every foul spirit, and a cage of every unclean and hateful bird.*" And so we add the warning uttered by "*another voice from heaven,*" "*Come out of her, my people, that ye be not partakers of her sins, and that ye receive not of her plagues.*"

Even if the plays could be so far reformed as not directly to cater to the vicious and the corrupt; if the foul birds of prey that perch aloft could be driven from the nests which they have occupied so long, still the theater would not be a good place of resort for those who feel that they possess immortal souls. The late hours, the expense of time and money, the character of the general audience, and the insensible and yet powerful effect of contact with them; the premature development and overgrowth of the passions, the distaste created for the quiet pleasures which are safest and best for soul and body, the rapidity with which the love of noise, show, and excitement becomes an overmastering passion, too strong to be controlled by duty, conscience, parental authority, or parental remonstrances and tears, conspire to render attendance at the theater ruinous to many and dangerous to all. Let no Christian go to the play-house even once. If the patronage of those who go but once, "just to see how it looks," could be wholly withdrawn, all the theaters would feel the loss, and some would be compelled to close their doors. Why should you make even one contribution to keep in motion the remorseless jaws which have devoured so many victims? Why should you lend your example, even once, to encourage the inconsiderate and the inexperienced to form the habit of attending the theater? Why consent to act, even once, as decoy duck, to lure many, it may be, to their destruction?

CHAPTER IV.

HORSE-RACING.

"*And so shall be the plague of the horse.*" Zech. xiv, 15.

THE horse is, doubtless, a noble beast; but, by some strange fatality, all sorts of thieves and cheats gather round him while living, as do the hungry crows when he is dead. Horse-racing may claim a place among popular amusements, since there is probably nothing, except an execution, more certain to attract a crowd. In many of the States of the Union horse-racing has been prohibited by law, because of the numberless evils connected with it, and the total absence of good. Within a few years, however, the thing has been revived under another name. State and county fairs are now held for the encouragement of agriculture, and specimens of various farm products are exhibited to edify the novice and quicken the zeal of the ambitious cultivator. Horses, of course, form a prominent feature of these exhibitions. But a horse can only be half seen till he is seen in motion, and so little "trials of speed," as they were delicately termed, were given just to add a little interest to the show. These trials of speed usurped more and more time and space, until they have in many cases swallowed up every thing else, and brought back the old-style horse-race, with its crowds, excitement, villainy, and vice of every kind, and, in fact, every thing but the name. An "Agricultural Fair" now means a plow, a pumpkin, a pig, and two hundred and fifty trotting horses. These fairs are almost invariably conducted with especial reference to the racing, and not unfrequently are engineered wholly by the jockeys themselves.

It will hardly do for us to adopt the sneering philosophy of Democritus, and find nothing but matter of merriment in the sins and follies of our fellow-men; nevertheless, these annual country gatherings have a comic side which one must be very blind not to see. The first note of preparation is the posting of immense placards, printed in as many colors as ever Joseph's coat knew, and offering premiums—ten cents for the best plow, five cents for the biggest pumpkin, twenty cents for the fattest pig, and one thousand dollars for the horse that can trot around a certain circle in the shortest time. Every gawky boy who rejoices in the possession of a long-legged colt, reads the flaming proclamation with delight, and straightway redoubles his diligence in training his colt and himself for the grand occasion. When the eventful day comes he presents himself on the spot, sure of winning the prize, and of seeing his name exalted in the county paper next week.

He finds nineteen other gawky individuals there with nineteen other colts and the same ambitious expectations. When they have paid their proportion of the money which is to become the prize, and have entered in a book the names of their horses—names, by the way, to devise which has cost many severe mental efforts—a strange man writes the name of a horse never before heard of in that locality. The contest proceeds. The strange man, who had been so still and taciturn up to this moment, suddenly discloses amazing energy, and shows himself an adept in all that pertains to the important business in hand. He knows tricks that make the astonished rustics open their eyes wide with admiration and dismay. He confuses his competitors with his bewildering maneuvers, secures every advantage, and urges on his own nag with a clamor and an uproar which drive the others into unlawful paces, or make them bolt from the track altogether. In short, science distances unsophisticated nature. The strange man and the strange horse sweep around the circle and rush to the goal in triumph, while the twenty are seen struggling far in the rear, a miserable conglomerate of dust, disappointment, and profanity. Meanwhile, the half-dozen secret confederates of the successful jockey have been quietly mingling with the crowd, betting with all who were willing to risk their money, and, of course, winning every time. Thus the concourse divide into three classes, like the notes in music; the *naturals* stare, the *flats* are fleeced, the *sharps* win. The performance being over, the professionals joyfully divide the spoil, praising with infinite glee "the way it was done," and venting their irrepressible hilarity in stentorian laughter and clumsy imitations of Indian war-dances.

The victims return home, the wiser ones satisfied with their recent experience, and determined to sell their sulkies and break their horses to the plow. The fools, on the other hand, are sure that now they know all about it. They have seen a professor of high art, and burn with ambition to be like him. They buy little caps of the same pattern, stick their hands in their pockets as nearly as possible in his style, and converse only in the phrases current in the stable. Their manners, as well as their clothes, smell strong of the horse. They devote their whole minds to the cause. They know more about the last race than the last war, and are more familiar with the names of fast trotters than with those of our great statesmen and generals. They can explain the pedigree of some favorite nag in a more satisfactory manner than they can their own, and take more pride in it. The tavern is the school where they pursue their professional studies, and the sages of the bar-room and the philosophers of the barn are their instructors. In some cases idleness, low company, and drink produce their natural fruit; the property inherited from the dead or dishonestly obtained from the living is soon squandered, the victim graduates as hostler, and, like some devotee of olden time, consecrates himself, soul and body, to the service of the brute which he admires. In others, the aspirant really reaches the high eminence at which he aims, and becomes a first-class cheat, learned in horse-craft and equally wise in the art of deceiving men—a restless operator in his chosen line of business, whose advent in a neighborhood is a signal for all to be on their guard, and at whose departure people breathe more freely.

The "Sports of the Turf," as they are called, are a mere compound of fraud and folly. Betting is the soul of horse-racing, and a thievish desire to get money without earning it is the soul of betting. How many "trials of speed" would there be if, by some method which man has never yet discovered, betting on the results could be wholly pre vented? Vice in all its forms—gambling, drunkenness, lying, cheating, profanity, rioting, and fighting—are the natural adjuncts of every race-course. Human birds of prey flock to it from under the whole heavens, and gorge themselves to the full. And with all this evil it has not one redeeming feature. As an amusement it is essentially low and animal. If two horses run a race, any body who is not an idiot knows that in all probability one will come out ahead of the other; and who but an idiot will care which it is? What matters it whether a horse that belongs to some branded swindler can go a mile in three minutes or two? Why should people leave their useful employments, and assemble in thousands, from far and near, merely to see one horse beat another horse? The whole thing is senseless.

While there is not a single solid argument in its favor, there are numerous and weighty objections against horse-racing. It involves a fearful waste. A race-horse is more expensive to keep than a family of ten children. The spectators who crowd to see the race lose time and money. The betting, inseparable from the affair, opens the flood-gates of a deluge of fraud and falsehood. It fires the hearts of the ignorant and inexperienced with that dangerous temptation, a thirst for money which they have not earned. The sudden losses and gains rouse the passions, and lead to collisions, fierce and furious, between losers and winners. The vender of intoxicating drinks will be there, for he knows that his chances are best when there is most of uproar and excitement. The professional pickpocket and the gambler will be there, for they know that the crowds will yield them a rich harvest of ill-gotten gain. The public roads in the vicinity of the race-ground will be dangerous to quiet travelers, by reason of the multitude of vehicles which dash along furiously, the drivers crazy with excitement and drink, and the horses wild with the shouting and the lash. And children will be there, their sensitive natures receiving impressions every moment, their eyes becoming accustomed to scenes of vice, and their ears familiar with the voice of passion and profanity.

The members of the Church of Christ should never be seen at such places. If one of them attending a horse-race should die there, by casualty or sudden disease, would it be considered good taste to name the locality in the funeral discourse? Would it figure well in the published obituary? The path of duty is so plain that none need err. Let no one, for a day or an hour, leave the rock and plunge into this abyss of fraud and folly. Besides the open, visible evils which cluster about a horse-race, there are great gulfs of villainy which few know of, and yet by which many suffer. Not seldom is the matter of victory and defeat secretly arranged days and weeks before the race takes place, and the men who make the treacherous compact win their tens of thousands by betting in favor of the horse which it is agreed shall distance the others. The habit of betting is a vice which speedily destroys all truth and honor. No amusement, so called, which lives by betting will long retain even the semblance of honesty. Horse-racing is certainly not an exception to this rule. Its whole history is black with treachery and fraud. No professed follower of Christ can have any thing to do with it, either in the way of active agency or secret encouragement, without sin.

We can not close this chapter more appropriately than by quoting the emphatic words of Thomas Hughes, an able member of the British Parliament and a decided friend of the American Republic. He had seen in the public journals the statement that certain capitalists of New York were about to establish somewhere on the Hudson a race-ground, which they hoped would, in time, rival the doubtful "glories of Epsom and Ascot:"

"Heaven help you! then; for of all the cankers of our old civilization there is nothing in this country approaching in unblushing meanness, in rascality holding its head high, to this belauded institution of the British turf.

"It is quite true that a very considerable section of our aristocracy is on the turf, but with what result? Shall a man touch pitch and not be defiled? There is not a man of them whose position and character has not been lowered by the connection, while in the majority it ends in bringing down their standard of morality to that of blacklegs, and delivering over their estates into the grasp of Jew attorneys.

"The last notable instance among oui *jeunesse doree* is that of the Duke of Hamilton, who succeeded to a clear £70,000 a year, some three years ago, and who is now a pensioner of his creditors in the ring, while the old palace of the Douglas is at the order and disposition of the celebrated Mr. Padwick. This gentleman, at his Derby dinner this year, entertained three dukes, two marquises, and six earls, and I believe there was only one untitled man at the board—all of these under the thumb or anxious to cultivate the esteemed favors of this 'giver of all good things.' Just consider for one moment what our modern system of betting has brought us to. A reliable *tip* is that which the most scrupulous young gentleman on the turf desires above all other earthly blessings before a great race; that is to say, some private information which may enable him to overreach his dearest friend or his own brother, if he can induce him to take the odds."

CHAPTER V.

BASE BALL.

"*And the people sat down to eat and drink, and rose up to play.*" Exodus xxxii, 6.

BASE BALL may be made a very pleasant amusement, wholly unobjectionable either in regard to health or morals. Many of our readers well remember how it used to be played by the village school-boys. Two of the best players volunteered, or were elected by acclamation, to organize the two "sides." The leaders tossed up a bat, with a mark on one side of it, to determine the first choice. The winner looked around the circle of boys and made his selection; then the other leader named a boy for his side, and so it went on, by alternate selections, till all were enrolled. The bat was again tossed up, to determine who should be "in" first, and then the play began. How they knocked the ball, and ran and threw the ball at each other, and fell down in their eagerness to avoid being hit, and laughed and shouted, and grew hot, and red, and finally weary! No crowd of excited spectators were there to applaud special acts of skill, and thus spoil the sport; no "scorer" noted down in his book the number of "runs" or of "fly-catches;" no representative of the public press was there, to prepare an extended and eloquent report, confounding simple readers with his vocabulary of new terms; no body inquired which side was victorious, and all were happy.

And in these later days, if a score of young men or older men would provide a basket of refreshments, and go out into the fields by themselves and play two or three hours, in the ancient and honorable way, carelessly, hilariously, not even noticing who makes the most "runs," they would all feel the better the next day; and the wit and humor elicited on the occasion would echo in twenty home circles for weeks to come.

But since it attained the dignity of being our "national game," base ball has become a ponderous and elaborate affair. Rules as rigid as those which govern the proceedings of the Congress of the United States are fixed, by general councils of men learned in the art, and goodly volumes are published discussing the size, shape, and weight of balls and bats, and determining the proper distances between the bases. Associations are formed, who assume a name, devise a uniform, and have initiation fees and monthly dues. The formation of the club, the selection of the members, is a very serious business, involving, as it does, the fortunes and the fame of the association in its future contests for championships and newspaper honors.

Young men are in demand who are willing to devote their whole time and mental en ergies to the acquisition of dexterity in throwing a ball or catching it. Professional players are found, who are recruited from that idle, shiftless, and yet ambitious class of mortals who are ready to work with the energy of giants one day in the week at any useless task, provided they have the privilege of lounging about the other six days, boasting of their feats and basking in the admiration of all the little boys in the neighborhood. These professionals train as carefully as prize-fighters, and are, in fact, the same style of men drawn mild. In some cases they hire themselves to the club for a single exhibition game; in others, they engage for the season. Their pay is ridiculously high, considering the service rendered. We hear of a club that secured one player for a thousand dollars for the season. Another player was induced to change his residence from one city to another, and was set up by his employers in a store, with a stock costing fifteen hundred dollars, by way of securing his valuable aid on great occasions.

When the club is organized, there must be daily practice for the benefit of the novices. This is done often to the neglect of every thing else, to the sore annoyance of parents and employers, and when a good degree of skill is supposed to be gained, another club, fifty or five hundred miles away, is invited to meet in friendly contest. The newspapers announce that the Exotics have challenged the Cupids, name the time and the place, and express an ardent hope that the weather will be propitious. The eventful day arrives; "play is called," and the contest proceeds with all spirit and vigor. They pitch, they bat, they run, they pant, they grow red in the face, they perspire, they strain their muscles and rend their garments in superhuman effort. The scorers set down their marks, the reporters of the public press scratch away at their notes, the spectators applaud. Intense excitement characterizes the entire performance. There is no brain power to spare on pleasantries, no surplus breath to waste in laughter. Awkward episodes occur. A head is broken by an erring bat, or a finger by a ball, or two players, running with upturned faces and outstretched hands to catch the same descending ball, rush together with a fearful thump, and fall backward in collapse. Perhaps proceedings are still further diversified by the occurrence of a little fight.

The game in due time ends, and one party or the other is declared victors by so many "runs," and the winners and the losers adjourn to a hotel and refresh themselves with a supper, of which wine-bibbing generally forms a prominent feature. Speeches, too, are made by the talking members of each club, expressive of the most intense admiration of each other's prowess, and breathing unutterable friendship. The reporter, who has been presented with a complimentary ticket for this very purpose, takes notes of what is said and done, and the next morning the newspaper lays before an admiring public the important intelligence that "the pitching of the Cupids was superb, the batting of the Exotics was magnificent, the fielding of Jones and Smith elicited universal applause, the supper was all that an epicure could desire, and the wit and eloquence of Mr. Brown's speech were equaled only by the beauty and pathos of Mr. Jenkins' reply." While an agitated world is laboring with this startling announcement, the principal performers stay at home and rest, or limp wearily out to the apothecary's to make investments in pain-killers and strengthening plasters.

And this, forsooth, is the great National Game. It has scarce a single feature of real recreation. The overwrought excitement, the excessive physical exertion, the absence of mental ease and conversational freedom condemn it. The publicity of the performance destroys all the good that might otherwise result from it, and, instead of play, makes it a mere exhibition, whose aim is not rest but notoriety, and whose effect upon the performer is not physical renewal but exhaustion. The game itself is not in fault. In its simple forms, pursued in moderation, with right associations, as a recreation, and not as an ambitious show, it can be heartily recommended to young men who need some active outdoor amusement. It may thus be made a very pleasant and not unprofitable thing. In its preposterous form, inflated into a "great national game," it is very laborious, very expensive in time and money, and not altogether safe for soul or body. It is then not an amusement, but a pretentious and useless display, whose highest reward is the shallow applause of the idle and the vain.

It may be hazardous to one's reputation

for sagacity to predict the downfall of any fashionable thing on the ground that it lacks the basis of good sense; still, I will say that the modern bubble has been blown so big, that it seems to me that it must collapse before long. If I mistake not, there are already signs of decay. Many young men, whose names are on the roll decline to play, and are active members of the club only at the supper-table. They pay their share of the expense of public games, and attend, but find it pleasant and politic to perch themselves daintily on the fence, to smoke and applaud in the shade, while their hired substitutes do the hard work in the hot sun. In due time the novelty of the whole thing will be gone, and then comes the end.

But if its having become an overgrown piece of folly were the only charge which may be made against it, base ball, even as cultivated by the clubs, might survive for a time. The expense is not in its favor. We know of a club where the regular annual dues are twelve dollars for each member. Besides this there is an initiation fee to be paid by beginners, and I presume extra expenses for extra occasions. The club has a hundred and fifty members, and the aggregate of regular dues can not be less than two thousand dollars a year. No doubt there are clubs whose annual expenditure amounts to three times the sum named. This certainly is a liberal price to pay for all the good gained.

There is, however, a much worse objection to base ball than the waste of money. The vices which cluster about the race-course begin to haunt the ball-ground. Thievish men find that bets can be made, and money lost and won, at a ball match as well as at a horse-race, and the same frauds and stratagems are employed. Sometimes money to the amount of fifty or even a hundred thousand dollars is staked on the result of a single match. Men do not need to bet large sums many times before they are ready for any trick, however infamous, which will enable them to win. We have seen, in a former chapter, how a horse-race is sometimes secretly sold beforehand, the parties to the fraud betting accordingly, and winning every thing. The same thing is not unknown, I am told, among the ball clubs. A match is in contemplation. A club of "champions" challenge another champion club, and all possible appliances and devices are employed to attract attention, draw a crowd, and create an excitement. While the rivals are apparently burning with intense desire for victory, and determined to contend for it with heroic energy, a few members of the clubs, without the consent or knowledge of the rest, agree so to manage that the victory shall go in a certain direction, and for a share of the spoils thus surrender the one side to premeditated defeat, and crown the other with false laurels. I have heard of one case, where a match game was played and many bets were pending, and interested parties secured a given result by paying the moderate sum of three hundred dollars.

In fact, so many vices are beginning to gather about the "great national game," as some foolishly term it, that every one connected with it seems to be regarded with a degree of suspicion. Merchants and others, who employ numbers of young men, are doubtful about members of ball clubs, and reject candidates who are connected with them. This looks a little hard, but we must remember that business men want reliable, trustworthy clerks, salesmen, and book-keepers. When we are trying to learn the character of a stranger every hint is of value, and a thing about which so many doubts cluster can not be a recommendation.

CHAPTER VI.

DANCING AND BALLS.

"*They send forth their little ones like a flock, and their children dance.*" Job xxi, 11.

LET us now turn from outdoor diversions to those amusements which do not, of necessity, demand daylight and space for their cultivation.

Dancing is one of these; and as attempts are being made at the present time to introduce it into circles whence it has hitherto been rigidly excluded, we honor it with the first place in this part of the discussion, and propose to give it all due attention. It is presumed that the advocates of dancing will insist, at the outset, that we shall make a distinction among the various fashionable dances of the times. It is not probable that any reader of this volume will attempt to defend the "German," or round dances. It is a shameful, revolting spectacle to see a young girl whirling around in the arms of a man who perhaps an hour ago was an utter stranger to her, her head leaning upon his breast, and their whole persons in closest contact. This style is positively immodest, corrupting, offensive to morals, as well as to delicacy and refinement. How dare a young man propose any such performance to a lady for whom he has a shadow of respect? How can any young lady, who respects herself, submit to it?

But cotillons and quadrilles, we are told, are different; they are modest, graceful, and harmless. Doubtless there is a difference, and yet they differ only as the varioloid differs from the worse disease.

It is not necessary to prove that the mere

motion is sinful in order to condemn it; nor need we assail the personal character of all who plead for dancing, in one form or another, as an innocent amusement. The abstract possibility of its being so practiced as to render it a healthful exercise may be admitted. I am acquainted with a gentleman of more than three-score years and ten, whose erect form and happy face, ruddy with health and radiant with kindness and inward peace, are pleasant to see. Meeting him in the street one day, I asked him how he managed to be young when he was old—how he contrived to keep up the life and bloom of Spring amid the chill winds and gathering clouds of Winter. In reply, he alluded reverently to the Divine Master, whom he serves in gladness of heart, as the source of all blessing, and then added: "I take care of my health. I take exercise. I rise early in the morning, and among the very first things that I do I put on a pair of soft slippers, go up into the attic of my house, and then go round and round in a circle, on a gentle run, till I am in a pleasant glow. This makes me feel well and cheerful all day."

Now, if any advocate of dancing will practice it only as our aged friend practices his peculiar exercise, we bring no accusation against his sanitary measures; we have no controversy with his principles or his performances. We will even go so far as to confess the beauty of certain fancy pictures of innocent dancing in the family circle, wherein one daughter presides at the piano, and the rest of the children whirl about in their graceful evolutions, till father and mother feel the happy contagion, and, starting up, join in the mirth; and even the white-haired grandsire looks on admiringly, and keeps time with his best foot, and applauds with his cane, and then calls the household to order for evening prayers. We do not happen to know any "happy family" where devotion and dancing live together on such excellent terms; nevertheless, extraordinary things do occur in the world, and this may possibly be among them.

But all this does not shake the settled conviction that it would be unwise to cultivate dancing of any sort as an amusement, or even to tolerate it. The reasons upon which this conclusion is based are numerous and weighty.

1. *Dancing as it is usually practiced, and will continue to be practiced, if at all, lacks the elements of true recreation.*

It is folly to talk of sending children to dancing schools, and then confine their performances to the family circle. Dancing is essentially an exhibition which addresses the eye of the spectator, and craves admiration. It tends directly to cultivate the love of display and of the praise which it elicits, a passion as avaricious in its way as the miser's greed of gold. Introduce dancing generally, and of the youth who attain a degree of proficiency not a few will soon tire of the approval of the little circle, and thirst for the applause of the multitude. They who imagine that they have acquired a grace and a skill which can not fail to win the praises of all beholders, will not be content to hide their light under the bushel of home, and soon the performances in the private parlor will be considered of no account, except as rehearsals for more public displays, and the ball-room will be looked upon as the proper field where artistic ambition is to win its laurels.

And in this form dancing is detrimental to soul and body. The late hours which it involves are a fatal objection to it. The confined atmosphere in which it is practiced is injurious. The style of the refreshments common on such occasions, and the untimely hour when they are taken, increase the evil. The undue excitement exhausts instead of invigorating the vital powers. The sudden transitions from the heated ball-room to the chill night air are not safe, as many an early grave can testify. These things conspire to make a ball or a dancing party a direct attack upon the health of those who attend it. Instead of invigorating the weak, it requires vigor to endure the exhausting strain. A single night thus spent will make its visible mark upon the face. They who escape with the least injury are languid and dull, and perhaps irritable, for days afterward, while some are totally unfitted for their usual avocations, and require time to recover, as if from an attack of illness. While physical health is thus impaired or imperiled, there is no promise of mental or moral improvement to compensate the injury. There is no time for rational conversation, and any attempt in that direction would be deemed out of place. The liveliest imagination can see no moral good in the performance. The whole thing produces no higher pleasure than engine-boys feel while running in search of the fire; and in the matter of aching heads and low spirits, it is probable that those who run with the engine and those who attend the ball are about alike the next day.

2. *Dancing has a bad historic name.*

There was, indeed, in ancient times, a solemn religious ceremony, which, through the poverty of human language, was called dancing. When Pharaoh and his host sank into the depths of the sea, while Israel stood safe upon the shore, Miriam and her maidens came forth with timbrels and with dances, and sang to the Lord a lofty anthem of praise and thanksgiving. When David brought home the ark of God he danced before it; but it was a strictly religious ceremony, nothing like the caperings and curvetings of our own day. There is no intimation whatever that Miriam and her maidens, or David, ever danced except on such occasions. Pleasure dances have been almost universally held in bad repute. The daughter of Herodias danced to please Herod, as he sat at the banquet, bewildered with wine; but the performer was one who could lightly ask for the life of an innocent man and a devoted servant of God; and the royal spectator was a tyrant, who could carelessly order his execution. In Rome, and Athens, and Ephesus the dancing was done by the degraded and the vile, who employed it as a means of advertising their profession. The dancers of Egypt and India at the present day are of the same character.

Now, I do not know that it would be right for me to denounce indiscriminately all who perform publicly in places of amusement in our cities and towns, yet it is safe for me to say that a dancing girl, however loudly her fame may be trumpeted by the newspapers, finds her professional reputation every-where a bar to her reception into good society. Why should it be so? It certainly is not because of the mere publicity of professional life. If it were, then Miss Dickinson and Miss Evans, and scores of others, would find themselves in the same condemnation, instead of being honored and applauded. Why a female public lecturer should be respected, and a female public dancer despised and shunned, I can not understand, unless there is something in dancing itself, or in the character of those who have made it their profession, that has merited condemnation. Ladies of the highest respectability go to hear the lecturer, and at the close crowd around the desk to be introduced to her; other ladies, certainly no more scrupulous in regard to their associations, go to see the dancer perform, and the next day will not look at her in the street. What makes the difference? Will the apologist for dancing explain?

3. *A love for dancing parties and balls is universally deemed inconsistent with the seriousness and devotion which characterize a true Christian.*

Dancing is regarded as the favorite diversion of the vain and the frivolous. Nominal Christians may be found at balls and dancing assemblies, but they are persons who have n weight of Christian character, and exert no influence in favor of religion. The world, unconvicted and careless, rather likes such professors of religion, because their example is an opiate wherewith to quiet an occasional pang of conscience. The worldly and the prayerless think more favorably of themselves and of their prospects of heaven when they see that Church members resemble them so closely. But when the worldly man is convinced of sin, and desires to find pardon, he never sends for one of these unfaithful professors to give him spiritual counsel. When the wicked are about to die, they do not want prayer offered at their bedside by any of these fiddling, dancing, wine-bibbing, honorary members of the Church. They name men and women of undoubted piety. They suspect those who can join them in their fol lies and feel no condemnation. They do not estimate very highly a Christian profession which exerts so little control over those that make it. Nay, rebuke a scorner for his sins, and in many cases he will seek to defend himself by a sneering allusion to those very professors of religion who verily believe that they were making capital for their Church by showing that it can not be suspected of being "Puritanic."

4. *Dancing involves undesirable associations.*

We bring no indiscriminate accusations against those who love to dance. In almost every community where it is cultivated to any great extent, it will not be confined to any particular class nor to any one moral level. Still, if we are to tell the whole truth, it must be stated that dancing prevails less as you ascend the scale of virtue, intelligence, and religion, and more as you go down to explore the realms of ignorance and vice. However numerous and, after their fashion, respectable its votaries may be, there is a line above which it never prevails. Like the deluge in the days of Noah, it fills the valleys first, and covers the low places; but, unlike the deluge, there are elevations which the swelling waters never reach, heights upon which the dark tide never shows even its spray. In our great cities, those sections which are recognized as the homes and dens of vice and degradation, the very region and shadow of death, abound in dance-houses; and the sound of the violin and of many trampling feet mingles nightly with the noise of rage and blasphemy, and the hoarse clamor of bloody strife. Intemperance and infamy are foul birds which agree well in the same nest with dancing. But as you ascend the scale, not only the more gross forms of vice, but the dance is left behind long before you reach the highest altitudes. The devotedly pious, the truly pure in heart, do not dance. In all ages of the Church such spirits have always kept aloof from the follies of their times, and had "no fellowship with the unfruitful works of darkness."

They who give themselves to this amusement, therefore, turn away from the best examples of pure and undefiled religion, and the noblest, holiest fellowship within their reach. They ally themselves with the worldly, the thoughtless, the prayerless, the gay butterflies of fashion and soulless pleasure. They throw themselves among influences in the highest degree unfavorable to sober views of life, and the earnest, thorough performance of its great duties. They voluntarily leave the rock and the shore of safety to launch upon a treacherous stream, the rippling music of whose waters will soon cease, and the bloom of whose flowery banks will soon disappear, and whose current, silent but swift and strong, bear them steadily away from light and hope down to despair, remorse, and ruin.

Dancing wastes time, wastes health, scatters serious thought, compromises Christian character, leads to entangling associations with frivolous minds and careless hearts. It is as sure a foe to intellectual growth as to moral progress. Young people who are famed as "beautiful dancers" are generally good for nothing else. The time that should be devoted to something valuable is spent in practicing posture-making before a mirror, or a professor of the high art, who shows them how to step so, and so, and so; while God calls, the Savior waits, life wanes, and the tremendous realities of the eternal world every moment come nearer. Even Cicero, the heathen moralist, affirms that "no man in his senses will dance." The dancing-master is the devil's drill-sergeant, just as the theater is the devil's church.

CHAPTER VII.

CARDS, CHESS, AND BILLIARDS.

"*Abstain from all appearance of evil.*" 1 Thess. v, 22.

CARDS are an old game—so old that it is impossible, not only to tell to whose ingenuity we may ascribe the useless invention, but even to name the land or the age in which they originated. They may be traced, however, to Asiatic sources. For many centuries the Chinese and the Hindoos have known the game, and from them it has spread over the world. It was cultivated by the Moors in Spain, and through their agency made its way into Italy, Germany, and the other nations of the West. In some European countries the pastime was prohibited by law. This prohibition probably grew out of the superstitions of the times, it being an article of popular faith that games of chance were under the control of the devil, who gave success to those who sold themselves to his service. But cards gradually came into favor among the idle and the frivolous; and at last even royalty—as royalty was in those days—did not disdain to indulge in them. Samuel Pepys, in his amusing and instructive diary, records that on a certain Sunday evening in February, 1667, he found Catherine, the Queen of Charles II, playing cards with the Duchess of York, and one or two more, the rooms being "full of ladies and great men." Addison, who wrote a little later, continually alludes to the game as the favorite diversion of the fashionables of his times; and such it seems to have continued among the gay and the thoughtless of English circles, till about the beginning of the present century. The love of it, however, was never universal.

Horne Tooke, who assailed the corruptions and tyranny of the English Government during the reign of George III, and was fined and imprisoned sundry times for his hardihood, was once introduced to the sovereign, who entered into a careless conversation with him, and, among other things, asked him if he played cards. "May it please your Majesty," was the witty reply, "I do not know a king from a knave."

It is said that cards are stealthily creeping up into circles from which they have hitherto been religiously excluded. And here the writer is constrained to confess his lack of personal knowledge of the subject under discussion. He is, indeed, aware that individual cards have their names, and are called kings and queens, knaves and spades; that they are "shuffled" and "cut," and that a certain something is called a "trick"—doubtless very appropriately—but having no ambition to stand in the presence of kings of this particular dynasty, no desire to cultivate the acquaintance of knaves of any sort, no love of tricks of any kind, he remains in willing ignorance even unto this day. Two or three times in the course of his life, he has seen people playing cards. First, one would lay down a piece of paper with spots on it, then another player would lay down another spotted paper, and so it went on so long as he beheld the performance; but the process did not seem to him to be attended by any particular result, nor did he learn, possibly because he did not wait and watch long enough, whether the victory depended most on chance, sagacity, or mathematical calculation.

But there are facts which every body knows. Cards are the gambler's tools. They are a favorite diversion of the aimless and the idle; they have a bad name among honest people If, as some say, they were introduced int(Europe by a physician, who adopted them as a means of diverting a royal patient whose intellect was shattered, we naturally infer that no great amount of intelligence, or strength of intellect, is needed to qualify the player. And to this inference it is not difficult to hang another—that the game is the fitting refuge of men and women who are conscious that their talents enable them to shine better in silence than in conversation. Whether, according to the rules of the play, a king is any better than a knave, or a diamond than a club, I do not claim to know, but I imagine that in playing, wit and intelligence find little more enjoyment than do the dullest and most stupid of the party.

One thing is certain, there is no true utility in the game. It invigorates neither body nor mind; it adds nothing to the store of mental wealth; and those ignorant of it lose nothing by their lack of knowledge. Again, it is certain that to some minds the game is dangerous. They are fascinated by it, led into doubtful associations and evil habits, and to ruin itself. It seems that the diversion is so barren of ideas, in itself so deficient in interest, that it becomes necessary to stake small sums of money "just to give it a little life." Thus the first step is taken in the road that leads to the gambler's hell, to the great joy of the demons who there watch for victims. Like other beasts of prey, professional gamblers can not live by devouring each other. Idleness must feed upon the earnings of industry or starve. Vice must burrow into the granary which belongs to virtue. The cool and calculating gambler will be delighted to see card-playing become fashionable among all classes of society. He knows that of those who begin with playing for mere pastime, a certain proportion will be bitten by the mania for playing for money, and thus be brought within reach of his remorseless claws.

One needs but little information in regard to card-playing to entitle him to the privilege of heartily despising it. Introduced, as it would seem, for the express purpose of reducing mental vivacity and culture to the same dead level with ignorance, it bears the semblance of an insult to any company in which it is proposed, wasting precious hours in a way which neither invigorates the body, nor supplies the mind with a single valuable idea. I do not see how any conscientious, intelligent person can deem it innocent. Fastening with a strange power upon characters of a peculiar make, and turning them into grist for the gambler's mill, no prudent person will deem it safe. Indeed, the history of every gambling den in the great cities of our own country, as well as in other lands, shows that the passion for cards, and the hope of winning money by them, often become an utter overmastering infatuation, almost worthy the name of insanity, which renders the victim reckless of the claims of honor, religion, and the tenderest affections of our nature, and drags him down relentlessly to his doom. Wholly barren of good results, prodigal of the precious time which God allots for nobler purposes, void of every element of rational recreation, to right minds unsatisfactory and to some minds unsafe, we need not wonder that the degree in which card-playing has prevailed at any given period of history, is a fair index of the corruption of the age. Let no professed follower of Christ defile his or her hands with so suspicious a thing.

CHESS claims to be a more intellectual, and even more ancient, game than cards. Its history and its principles have been set forth in goodly volumes. Poetry has sung its charms. The lives of its famous players have been written and their methods described, and a whole library of its peculiar literature has grown up around it. Its admirers trace its history for five thousand years, and inform us that it originated among the acute, dreaming inhabitants of India. The chess-player plumes himself on the aristocratic character of his favorite amusement, as if it placed him above the level of common mortals.

In some points chess is less objectionable than cards. It does not depend on chance, and there is little opportunity to cheat. Moreover, where the players are skillful, it requires a long while to complete a game. For these reasons, as I suppose, chess has never been adopted, so far as I can learn, by the professional gambler; and, therefore, its historic name and present social standing are better. Mind challenges mind, and skill alone wins the victory in the duel of intellect. Chess is not likely to become epidemic. It is so deep a game; it demands so much of time and silence for the contest; it employs so small a number at once, that the gay and the thoughtless, who are in most danger from irrational amusements, will care little for it. Still, if the reader needs a hint, and is glancing along these pages in search of it, he may weigh the suggestions which follow.

8

Nobody who assumes to play chess at all is willing to be known as a poor player. To play well, or even respectably, involves a great deal of study and practice, and the spending of much time and mental energy; enough, in fact, to learn one of the dead languages. The game so taxes the intellect that it can not be resorted to as a relaxation from mental toil. There is no physical exercise in it, no courting of the sunlight and the breeze; therefore, it can not be made a good recreation for the sedentary. It conveys no new ideas, makes no additions to our accumulations of mental treasure; and, therefore, it is a poor business for those who need their leisure hours for mental improvement.

Chess is not popularly a recreation, but a *pastime;* that is, a way of passing the time; and the time thus passed is wasted. Many a man, bewitched with chess, which has left his mind unfurnished and his heart untouched, has spent over it precious days and years, which, if rightly improved, would have made him intelligent, wise, and greatly useful in his generation. They who fear God ought not thus to waste the golden moments. If th regular duties of the day leave certain hours at our disposal, these hours are too valuable to be dreamed away over a painted board, and a handful of puppets. The sedentary need air and active exercise, which will expand the lungs, and clothe the whole frame with strength. Those whose labor is chiefly that of the hands, need books and newspapers. The student, the clerk, the apprentice, the daughter at home, have more important "moves" to make than those of the chess-board, a wiser way to employ brain power than to spend it on a laborious nothing, a better warfare to wage than the petty antagonisms of useless skill, a record to make in the Book of Life worth infinitely more than a life-long shout of this world's shallow praise of checks and champions.

Billiards are simply big marbles, "only this and nothing more." Authorities on the subject inform us that the table for playing the game must be twelve feet long, and six feet wide, the top being of slate, covered with cloth. Around the raised edges are cushions of India rubber, and sundry pockets. Instead of employing his thumb and fingers to shoot his marble, as in the original game, the billiard player uses a stick. There are two sorts of sticks—a long one called a cue, and a short one termed a mace. One writer confesses that the cue is the thing, and the only thing, for the expert to use; but advises ladies to be content with the mace, "since to execute finely with the cue sometimes requires the assumption of attitudes which are not becoming female attire, or to the modesty of the sex." Just so. By all means, let the ladies, however ambitious, stick to the mace, even if it is "considered merely as the implement for novices." Perhaps we ought to condole with the ladies on the distressing dilemma in which this places them. The mace confesses awkwardness; the cue is forbidden. They are doomed to remain forever novices in the high art, or sacrifice delicacy to ambition.

But what is the game? The expert player places his hand on the table a few inches from the ball, and resting his cue upon it and bending over to look along the stick, studies the situation with the motionless attitude and fixed gaze of a hungry toad taking aim at a fly. Then with the end of his stick he strikes the ball, which, if his calculations are correct, goes in a certain direction, hits another ball, and then goes somewhere else. And this is all. It is true, to be able to make the ball go exactly in the right direction, and stop at the right point, requires, as our author declares, "immense practice;" yet the highest achievement attainable is to cause one marble to hit one or two others, and drop into a pocket.

This statement of the true character of the

game is about all that needs to be set forth to condemn it among intelligent, thoughtful people. It has nothing in it to inform, refine, or in any way improve the mind. The only mental faculties cultivated are those which judge of distances, angles, and muscular forces. To aim at skill is to sacrifice months and years of valuable time to a very mean ambition. It is the favorite device of the saloon and the grog-shop, the bait to entice men from their homes in the evening, and keep them till midnight, drinking, smoking, and telling indecent stories. There is method and design in the pother which the newspapers make over matches and champions, as if the honor of nations were involved in the success of those who volunteer to represent them in petty contest. It is expected that the idler and the spendthrift will be attracted to the place; and in the crowd the seller of alcohol will find customers, and the swindler victims. Billiards figure very low in the scale of amusements. Associated as it generally is with late hours, confined air, smoking and drinking, the game is detrimental to health, to morals, and to mind. Kept clear of evil associations, there is nothing in it to attract the intelligent and the thoughtful. And seeing that the righteous are generally called home when their work is done, the professor of religion, who can find nothing better to do than play billiards, need not expect to live long.

CHAPTER VIII.

NOVELS AND NOVEL-READING.

"*Of making many books there is no end.*" Eccl. xii, 12.

WHAT is a NOVEL? A recent writer thus defines it: A novel is a portraiture of "something new falling within the domain of fancy or imagination, with its interest centering in love." If this be correct, it would seem that a novel, as such, is neither good nor bad, but is the one or the other according to its own individual character. To portray something new is certainly not wrong if the portraiture be true, and there be a good reason for the portrayal. There is a place, also, for fancy and imagination in the legitimate operations of the mind; nor does the fact that the interest centers in love necessarily condemn it. True love, such as God designed to exist among the families of men, is a golden chain which binds in the best and purest friendship known on earth. Genuine, honest, rational love needs to be cultivated, not rebuked and repressed. It needs the controlling and formative influences of intelligence, reason, and religion, and may, therefore, be discussed by the press and on the platform or even in the pulpit.

And yet novel-reading has become one of the great vices of our age. Multitudes care for nothing but light reading. The bookstores abound with works of fiction. The records of our public libraries show that there are more readers in this department than any other—perhaps more than in all the rest. The literature which finds its way into the hands of our people, as they journey by land or water, is almost invariably fictitious. Our weekly periodicals, secular and religious, often have their serial story. Our Sunday school libraries have been overwhelmed by the flood of weak and washy literature till scarce a vestige of sober history or real biography shows itself above the surface of the wild wilderness of waters. A whole generation of young people are growing up, to whom solid books are unknown, to whom the great historic names of the past are but a sound, and whose ignorance of the world of fact is poorly compensated by their acquaintance with the world of dreams.

It is a rule in political economy that demand creates supply. As all kinds of readers addict themselves to fiction, so all sorts of writers press into this wide and productive field, and exhibit results of every degree of badness, with now and then something of better quality. It is not easy for the young to find their way through this labyrinth of good and evil, the good little and the evil infinite. The safest rule, in whose application the fewest mistakes will be made, is that of TOTAL ABSTINENCE. To declare that all the wild fruit of a certain forest is poisonous, and to prophecy the death of every one who eats a single berry there, may be contrary to truth; nevertheless, if nine out of ten of the kinds found there are deadly, and none but a well-taught observer is able to distinguish between the good and the evil, the warning to be given to the inexperienced is, "Touch not, taste not."

In regard to novels this is often the only available rule. But if we are required to give more discriminating advice, there are four maxims which are plain, and, if faithfully adhered to, will, I think, be found safe.

1. *If you have but little time for reading, spend none of it on works of fiction.*

Your success in life, your happiness, usefulness, and safety in the world depend upon your intelligence, your good sense, your moral character, your modes of living. What you are to be and what you are capable of accomplishing will depend, in no small degree, upon what you know. You require solid information. You need to learn ten thousand things which are to be found in books. Your usefulness in the circles to which you belong and your position in the community are intimately connected with the degree in which you improve your mind. You have much to do. You have no time to waste on counterfeit coin while golden treasures of knowledge woo you on every side. Read your Bibles. Read history, the records of the past, and the accounts of current events. Read the biographies of good men and women. Read books of science. Push your researches in every direction, delve in every mine that opens before you. Traverse every rich field that invites your footsteps. Discipline your mind, store your memory; train your will to all high resolves. If your lot in life is such that little time can be given to intellectual culture, do not waste an hour on the idle dreams of the novelists.

2. *In any case read only the best works of fiction.*

Supposing that the time which you are able to devote to books is not narrowed down to an occasional leisure hour, and you feel disposed to glance at the department of fiction, read only the best. Books are companions. Choose your company wisely. Where a multitude surround you, the pious and the profane, the virtuous and the vile, the refined and the brutish, it is madness to associate with all that come. You know what the effect upon your good name would be if you were seen walking arm in arm with those whose very presence is dishonor. There are books so vile that the mere possession of them is fatal to reputation. You will find people whose minds are so empty, and whose talk is so frivolous, that the time spent in their society is lost. There are many books of the same sort. You will meet still other people with whom you can not spend an hour without feeling that you have learned something worth knowing, that you have received an impulse in the direction of the true, the beautiful, and the good, and that you are wiser, purer, stronger because of the interview. There are books of this kind also. For the same reason, then, that you keep the best company to which you have access, read the best books within your reach. They will influence you as certainly as will living associates.

There are some few works of fiction which are well written and true to nature, and which inculcate the right and condemn the wrong. If you read fiction at all, read these. I do not name them, because I am not willing to be held responsible for all the time which might possibly be spent over them on the plea that they are here recommended. If you do not know which they are, you will lose nothing by waiting till you are better informed. As for the bad, their "name is Legion."

3. *In all cases let works of fiction form but a very small part of what you read.*

Read only the best, and read only a few even of the best. Or, if you want a more definite rule, read ten good, substantial works to every one of fiction, however good. The best works of imagination go but a little way in supplying the mental aliment which you need. You can not live on the odor of flowers, nor build up strong bone and muscle out of rainbows and moonbeams. You will grow in intelligence, sense, virtue, practical power for good only by means of solid food. Portraitures of "something new, falling within the domain of fancy, with their interest centering in love," may please for the moment, but if you get nothing better your soul will be as poor and lank as the lean kine of Pharaoh's dream. Confining your reading of this sort to the least objectionable of the class, you must add another restriction, in order to be safe, and confine the time thus spent to your leisure moments—what remains after you have given due attention to better things.

4. *Cease wholly to read fiction the moment you find that it begins to render substantial reading distasteful, and the common duties of life irksome, or injure you in any way in mind or morals.*

The man who has tampered with some intoxicating drug until an artificial want, a new, imperious appetite, has been created, is on the road to ruin, so they have already done themselves a fearful wrong who have indulged in the intoxications of fiction, until they are restless and unsatisfied without it, and unostentatious every-day life, such as belongs to the vast majority of mortals, seems tame, dull, void of interest, so that the mind can with difficulty be held to its common-place details and duties. And the same question may be made a test in both cases. What effort will it cost to stop? Will it require a mighty struggle, an agony of soul, a summoning of all concentrated power of will? Then summon the power and form the high resolve without a moment's delay, for life and death tremble in the balance. Are virtue and honor so far undermined that the victim is ready to take refuge in hypocrisy and lies, denying in public and indulging in secret? Alas! it is to be feared that the work of ruin is already done. At all events, only one hope remains. There must be a quick and thorough reform, a sudden sundering of the chains which bind to the "body of death." In the matter of novels, are you uncertain whether the point of peril has been reached in your own case? Try yourself. Lay aside light reading; take up some solid work, and see if you can so interest yourself in it that you keep on to the end without impatience, without a temptation to hurry over the tiresome task. If, like the Hebrews in the wilderness, you find it a weary march through a dry land, where you are haunted at every step by the recollection of the savory flesh-pots which you have left behind you, be assured that you can not escape too soon. The real question is whether you are not too far gone to escape at all. Error in regard to the reading of fiction is fraught with so many evils, that the rules given, stringent as they may seem, are abundantly justified.

Let our young people be constantly on their guard against the mental enslavement which marks the confirmed novel-reader. Common novel-reading is a fearful evil, and against it there are arguments numerous and weighty, which all will do well to heed.

1. *It wastes precious time.*

By universal consent, works of fiction are called "light literature;" and the name is correctly applied. To produce them belongs to light thinkers, men and women whose purposes, principles, and convictions are all light—the light-weights of the world of mind and morals. How strangely the name of Martin Luther, John Wesley, or George Washington would sound connected with the authorship of a fanciful story whose "interest centers in love!" The names which illumine the historic page with the purest light are those which it would amaze us to find connected with the authorship of ordinary fiction. It is worth while to pause and inquire why we would be surprised. Is not this the solution: that men of real greatness, working in thorough earnest, under the influence of profound conviction, are too busy with the events and duties of the age in which they live to find time to spin out of nothing a dream life for the amusement of idle minds?

It is evident that but little is gained by the instructions of teachers so inferior as are the great mass of novel-writers. Their productions are too easy reading to discipline the mind. They aim chiefly to amuse the reader, not instruct, nor convince, nor raise him to the height of a great purpose; and, in general, the best that can be said of the best of them is, that they confer pleasure without inflicting injury. But whatever may be the quality, you may be sure that excess in quantity is injurious. The vast majority of novel readers are young, and for them to squander the precious hours is suicidal. Youth, wasted, ushers in a feeble middle life and an unhappy old age. They who sow nothing in the Spring will lament over an Autumn which brings no fruit. Novel-reading is simply a diversion, a pastime, and to spend more than an occasional hour in diversion, however innocent it may be in itself, is a waste of time, too precious to be thus thrown away.

2. *Excessive light reading injures the mind.* The novelist seeks to bear his readers along without any labor on their part. They simply

witness the action, and watch the unfolding of the plot. The author amuses them with wit and humor; and, if he can, melts them with pathos, or charms them with eloquent description. He is the performer, and they are the spectators. If he is one of the best of his class, they may improve a little in some branches of knowledge, provided they are content to read slowly enough for the purpose. But habitual novel-readers hurry on to see "how it all comes out," seldom pausing to consider the force of a figure, or the beauty of an expression. Ingenious thought, keen discrimination in depicting character, accurate descriptions of natural scenery, nice points of style, are lost in the rush of words. There is a headlong race of event after event, shadows and light, storm and calm, and at last an end, a rapid panorama, little of which is seen distinctly while it is passing, and still less is remembered when it is past. The intellect does not grow strong playing with straws thus, where there is no exercise of the judgment on what is read, no effort of the memory to retain any thing. The novel-reader that does little or nothing but lounge about with a weak dilution of literature in hand, will soon become as soft and flabby in mind as in muscle, wholly incapable of lofty purposes and worthy deeds.

3. *Excessive light reading tends to unfit for real life.*

A devourer of novels seldom has an appetite for any thing else. To do our duty well, we must have our thoughts upon it, and our minds interested in it. The heart and the hands must go together, or the hands will soon tire, and do their work indifferently. What chance is there for the student who indeed holds Blackstone or Wood before his dreamy eyes, but whose thoughts are upon the unfinished romance in his desk? How can the daughter at home find happiness in aiding to bear the burden of domestic cares, while her mind is in a whirl over some delicious love-story, in which she has lost her identity in that of the fascinating Lady Something, with four desperate rivals for her hand, and the crisis of her fate just over-leaf?

Works of fiction would be less doubtful reading if the reader, after finishing the last page of the story, utterly forgot the whole, or remembered it only as we remember veritable history. The loss in that case would be chiefly loss of time. But as things are, novel-readers spend many a precious hour in dreaming out clumsy little romances of their own, in which they themselves are the beautiful ladies and the gallant gentlemen who achieve impossibilities, suffer unutterable woe for a season, and at last anchor in a boundless ocean of connubial bliss. Nor does it require much previous mental cultivation to enable one to indulge in these visionary joys. The school-boy and school-girl, the apprentice, the seamstress, the girl in the kitchen, can conjure up rosy dreams as readily as other people; and perhaps more readily, as it requires but little reading of the sort to render them impatient of their lot in life, and set them to imagine something that looks higher and better.

In fact, the Cinderella of the old nursery story is the true type of thousands of our novel-readers. They live a sort of double life—one in their own proper persons, and in their real homes; the other as ideal lords and ladies in dream-land. Ella, sitting among her native cinders, is a very prosaic individual, addicted to exceedingly prosaic employments, and fulfilling a destiny far removed from sublimated romance. But touched by the wand of the good Fairy, Ella is transfigured, her coarse garments are robes of magnificence, the mice are prancing steeds, the pumpkin is a coach, and she rides in state, the admiration of all beholders, and weds the prince triumphantly.

The modern Ella, sitting among the cinders, has indeed no good Fairy to confer sudden splendors upon her; but her place is well supplied by sundry periodicals, designed for just this style of readers. And so Ella invests her six cents weekly, and reads, and dreams. According to the flesh, she bears an honest, humble name, busies herself with a cooking stove, or a noisy sewing-machine, and with all her matrimonial anglings, perhaps has never a nibble. In her other capacity she is the Countess of Moonshine, who dwells in a Castle of Spain, wears a coronet of diamonds, and to whom ardent lords and smitten princes make love in loftiest eloquence; and she is blest. But, as Napoleon once observed, there is only a step between the sublime and the ridiculous. At any moment the coach of state may relapse into its original squash, the prancing horses again become mice, the costly array turn once more to rags; and the Countess, sweeping in her trailing robes through the glittering crowd of admiring lords and envious ladies, subside into her former simple self, with the hideous onions to be peeled, or the clattering machine to be kept in motion.

How can the two parts of this double existence harmonize? How is it possible for those whose minds are thus bewildered, and who have formed this inveterate habit of indulging in sentimental reverie, to engage heartily in the performance of commonplace duties? The inevitable result of excessive novel-reading is a distaste, if not an incapacity, for the sober thought and patient effort which are the price of success in every worthy path of life.

4. *Excessive novel-reading creates an over-growth of the passions.*

The novel-reader naturally, and perhaps unconsciously, becomes identified with the personage in the story who is nearest to what he or she would like to be. With the book in his hand, and his whole soul for the time being wrapped up in the exciting history, the young man ceases to be the apprentice, the clerk, the student, the farmer's boy, the plain John or Peter of his real self. He is merged in the hero of the story, handsome in person, brilliant in mind, endowed with every excellence, and bearing a name of at least three syllables. He becomes the ardent suitor of the beautiful lady, the heiress of the immense estate. The burning words in which love is portrayed are his words. The whole thing becomes so far a reality that it has something of the force of a genuine experience; and he feels happy, or grows melancholy with the varying fortunes of his imaginary passion.

Now, if Peter be a boy of fifteen, it is tolerably evident that he is advancing a little too fast in his sentimental career. Like a certain variety of pears described in the fruit books, there is danger of his being rotten before he is ripe. He is meditating matrimony when he has scarcely got beyond the limits of marbles and green apples. He looks around at the little girls to see which of them is the princess in disguise; and soon imagines that he is desperately in love with some little damsel in the neighborhood, and seeing that in this dreadful world disappointment is always possible, he begins to canvass the most picturesque and pathetic modes of committing suicide, in case the ferocious uncle should interfere, as he did in the book.

The young lady is similarly affected. She fancies herself the beautiful heroine of the story, rich, accomplished, and, romantically, wretched. She, too, begins to look about for the model lover who lays his hand upon his heart, lifts his tearful face toward heaven, and says pretty things. She feels disdain for the plain young men of her acquaintance, and perhaps fixes her eyes upon some flashy stranger, whose unknown antecedents give her a chance to invest him with all the impossible perfections her romantic fancy is able to invent.

Now, this state of things has its ridiculous side, but it is not healthy nor safe. The effects are too serious to be passed by with a smile. The inveterate habit of day-dreaming thus created absorbs the thoughts, destroys the mental balance, impairs sound judgment, and produces tendencies which are very far from the views and feelings, aims and principles, on which usefulness and honor in the world depend. There is an overgrowth of the passions, an exaltation of marriage out of all due proportion to other sources of rational happiness, an overestimate of beauty, wealth, and the other accidentals of human life; and a corresponding underestimate of the value of piety, industry, and the sober virtues which are "in the sight of God of great price." It is a vice of novelists as a class, to exalt love and matrimony above all else, and thus create in susceptible youth the habit of thinking and dreaming of matrimony above all else. Thus the novelist literally "turns the heads" of young people, inasmuch as he places foremost and uppermost the faculty which the phrenologists locate low down in the back of the brain.

5. *The habit of novel-reading creates a morbid love of excitement somewhat akin to the imperious thirst of the inebriate.*

The victim of drugs does not love opium or alcohol because of its taste or smell. The effect which he covets is, in truth, a mental effect. He resorts to the drug that he may feel rich, powerful, exalted, and happy, while, in reality, he is "wretched, and miserable, and poor, and blind, and naked." The victim of novels aims at the same thing in another way, by applying the bane directly to the mind itself.

But the inebriate soon finds that in order to produce the desired effect he must, from time to time, increase the strength of the dose. He adds to the quantity. Then from wine he goes on to brandy, and from that to absinthe, drugging his benumbed brain to the verge of death, to gain, from time to time, a feeble return of the momentary joys which once a very little of his chosen stimulus had power to impart. The experience of the confirmed novel-reader is similar. The simple tales of innocent love which interest the beginner soon become commonplace. They fail to excite the fancy or stir the emotions, and then something stronger must be had. Quiet love and ordinary incident must give place to fierce rivalry and jealousy, hate, revenge, and murder.

The editors of certain periodicals belonging to this style of literature seem to have decided that the public mind in general has reached this final stage. I confess that my knowledge of these periodicals is not extensive, being confined to what is gained by passing glance at windows and hand-bills, where their pictorial baits are thrust out to entrap buyers. The pictures which greet the eyes of passengers are almost invariably pictures of somebody shooting or stabbing somebody. The last embellishment which I have noticed, however, is a cut of somebody strangling the other somebody with his naked hands. This is doubtless still more delightfully horrible to the admirers of this style of writing, and calculated to thrill them with a new sensation. When the mind has become so vitiated that it turns away not only from all solid reading, but even from the less objectionable works of fiction, to revel in nauseous descriptions of lawless passions and bloody deeds, and is so besotted with them that every thing else is void of interest, and every duty irksome, how far is it removed from some of the worst evils of drunkenness or even of insanity itself? How much worse is the victim of alcohol or opium than the victim of mental intoxication?

6. *The habitual reading of novels tends to lessen the reader's horror of crime and wickedness.*

Crime is seldom actually committed until the mind has become familiar with the thoughts of it. The books which picture passion and crime keep the readers in closest contact with evil till the horror with which they first shrank from it is gone. Moreover, these books are sometimes written to serve a special purpose. An author may be given to some sin which places him under the ban of respectable society. He grows restive and malicious under the frowns of the good. He writes a book in which his own vice is white-washed into a sort of semi-respectability, and made merely an amiable weakness, while some Church member of sounding professions, or perhaps a Christian minister, turns out to be the villain of the plot. Thus in one character we see a villain bearing the Christian name, and in another a gross vice united with so many shining qualities that the moral deformity is hidden by the splendors that are thrown around it. Thus the reader is trained to look suspiciously upon the virtuous and smile upon the vicious. If he is tempted in the direction of any particular wickedness, his memory will easily supply him with some model from the books, who was given to the same thing, and was a noble character, nevertheless, the admiration of all about him, generous, brave, and in the end successful and happy. The inference of the tempted one is naturally this: that he too can yield and be admired, and in the end be happy.

Aside from the fictitious respectability which vice gains by being portrayed as not incompatible with the possession of high and generous qualities, needless familiarity with the idea of crime lessens the horror with which we regard it. The more suicides in any community the more easy it is to commit suicide, when rage and disappointment supply the temptation. In communities where every man goes armed, and every eye is familiar with scenes of blood, small provocations lead to murder. It is not irrational to assume that one reason why play-actors, as a class, tend to low morals is because it is a part of their regular business to personate immoral characters on the stage; and when the mind has become thoroughly imbued with the idea, and the lips familiar with the language of wickedness, the step from shams to reality is short and easy.

Thus the press becomes an apostle of unrighteousness when it lends its power to make the public mind familiar with all the phases of depravity. He that delights to dwell upon the nauseous details is not morally safe, and the vice which furnishes his choice reading is the very one into which he is liable to fall. The refined and the pure shrink with loathing from needless contact with the things which they condemn and abhor. I believe that the fearful multiplication of tragic crimes in our own day is due, in no small degree, to two causes—one the too general circulation of a corrupt literature, which familiarizes the reader with all that is detestable and infamous in character and conduct, the other the common use of drugged liquors, which fire the brain with a wilder frenzy than even that which is produced by alcohol, and drive men to their doom with a still more powerful, relentless force. In brief, the increased prevalence of gross forms of wickedness is due to a general poisoning, mental and physical, which fills the minds and the veins of its victims with a more deadly venom than we have hitherto known.

An extract from a religious periodical, which comes to hand while I am writing, corroborates the first part of the statement made.

"A young man—J. H. W.—committed suicide recently in Indianapolis. He left a letter to his brother, in which he says: 'I believe that if I had never read a novel I should now be on the high road to fortune; but, alas! I was allowed to read the vilest kind of novels when I was eight or nine years old. If good books had been furnished me, and no bad ones, I should have read the good books with the same zest that I did the bad. Persuade all persons over whom you have any influence not to read novels.' The Ordinary of Newgate Prison, in his report to the Lord Mayor, represents what a fruitful source of crime the Jack Sheppard and Paul Clifford style of novels has been among the youth of England. Inquiring into the causes which brought many lads of respectable parentage to the city prison, he discovered that all these boys, without one exception, had been in the habit of reading those cheap periodicals which are now published for the alleged instruction and amusement of the youth of both sexes."

7. *Excessive devotion to fictitious reading is totally at variance with Scriptural piety.*

This needs neither proof nor illustration. Genuine piety takes hold of the heart, and draws the thoughts and the affections toward God, and makes duty the source of the sweetest enjoyment. But when the novel usurps the place of the Bible; when secret prayer is hurried over, or wholly neglected, because of a burning desire to know what comes next in the story; when meditation on divine things is forgotten in endless day-dreams of love and worldly splendor; or, worse still, when real life is thrown into the shade by the unreal, and made to appear mean and insipid; when the action of conscience and sober reason is swept aside by the wild delirium of mental intoxication, what result can we look for save apostasy and final ruin?

While I contemplate these things, I confess that I am almost ready to recant the former part of this chapter, and insert in the place of it a rigid iron rule for the guidance of all, young and old, learned and unlearned: TOTAL

ABSTINENCE FROM NOVEL-READING HENCEFORTH AND FOREVER. Surely, there is abundant cause for the rule of the Methodist Episcopal Church, which warns all her communicants to abstain from "reading those books which do not tend to the knowledge or love of God."

CHAPTER IX.

SOCIAL GATHERINGS.

"*How can one be warm alone?*" Eccl. iv, 11.

TIME would fail me to examine the numerous and diversified amusements practiced in various parts of our land. Some are local; others are known every-where. Some are right and wise; some are otherwise. Some are intellectual and refined; others are mere noisy romps. Of many of the older sort the chief end was *kissing*. This latter feature may not have been particularly objectionable in little neighborhood gatherings in the country, where every body had known every body else all their lives, and half the young people in the room were cousins. The reader, however, will doubtless agree in the opinion that in more general assemblies it is not over refined, and may well give place to something else of less doubtful propriety.

To go through the whole list of these diversions, and pronounce upon the merits of each, would be tedious and useless. My aim has been to discuss principles, and then, in the light of those principles, to examine some of the more objectionable diversions now pleading for popular favor. If those principles are as plain as I take them to be, it will not be difficult to apply them to any new candidate for our suffrages. The reader, nevertheless, may object to an abrupt close of the discussion. He may say that this series of trials and condemnations is not enough, and that he is now waiting to be informed in regard to the recreations which are allowable and right; that having been warned against the forbidden fruit, he would now like to see the other trees, of which he may freely eat.

The suggestion is not without force; and yet it will require but a moment's reflection to make it clear that I can not comply with it. To attempt to make a mere list of the names of rational recreations would, for many reasons, be unwise. In some cases games and amusements are local, and to readers belonging elsewhere the mere name would convey no information. The same name is also applied to different diversions in different localities, and, therefore, approval or censure would be misunderstood and misapplied. It is evident that a simple list of amusements to be condemned, and another list of those approved, would be of little service.

On the other hand, if I should attempt to escape misconstruction by describing fully the amusements condemned or approved, the whole plan of this little volume would be changed, and it would become properly a Book of Diversions instead of a discussion of principles. That such a work might be written—possibly not in vain—is not denied; but it is no part of my plan to write it. Nevertheless, I do not hesitate to offer a few practical suggestions.

Permit me to say, first of all, that if any of my readers have nothing useful to do—no solid purpose in life, no proper employment, nor desire for any—they are counted out of this discussion. The idle, the frivolous, the useless have no right to recreation. They must reform their aimless, empty lives, and by industry earn the privilege of rest and relaxation before they are entitled even to hold an opinion on the subject. Let me add that no diversion, no amusement can impart more than a momentary pleasure to the indolent and the listless. A degree of hunger alone can prepare a man fully to enjoy his food. It is the sleep of the laboring man that is sweet. True recreation involves the idea of rest; relief, pleasant change of occupation. So the active, the busy, the industrious alone truly enjoy recreation. They who make amusement their only pursuit will soon find it utter weariness. For such I have only pity, and for them I am not writing.

But the active and the industrious, who "redeem the time," are entitled to their hours and modes of recreation. So far from denying it to be their privilege, I proclaim it to be their duty. The time and the manner must, of course, be adapted to their varying circumstances. The school-boy and school-girl need active exercise out-of-doors, in the light of the sun, else they are liable to grow up colorless and spindling, like vegetables which have sprouted in the cellar. Every one, older or younger, whose mind toils while the muscles are inactive, needs the sunbeams and the breeze. They whose employment, on the contrary, taxes the muscles, while the mind is comparatively inactive, require modes of recreation which spur the intellect, quicken the imagination, and store the memory with rich treasures of thought. Those whose daily avocation confines their thoughts to a narrow circle must find a wider range elsewhere, and exercise their wings in longer flights. They who work alone and in silence, need society; and those spending much of their time in a crowd will profit by an occasional hour of quiet, solitary meditation. It was a curious habit of the late Dr. Archibald Alexander, of Princeton, to spend the hour of evening twilight alone in his study, sitting in silent thought amid the deepening shadows. Who will say that it was not wise? What lofty argument, what profound knowledge of spiritual things, what emotions of divine love and adoration may not have been drawn thus from the well of silence and quiet waiting?

The chief recreation of the world at large is *conversation*. Talking is the joy of the whole earth. It is one of the great employments of life. Our utterances are often more important—do more good and evil than our deeds. All human wisdom, knowledge, sentiment, wit, fancy, flow in the channel of speech. By words truth conquers, reforms progress, mind acts upon mind, heart reaches heart, soul converses with soul. The lips may utter golden speech, or drip with the poison of asps. Human breath can come like the breezes of Paradise, or blast like the deadly sirocco of the hot desert. Aside from the deep joy of worship, and the hope of eternal life, there is no happiness, purer, richer, better than that which springs from words. And there is little true recreation which does not make conversation one of its chief features, and rely upon it as its great charm.

Conversation implies social life. And here, in regard to social gatherings, I will make a suggestion which I am persuaded that my readers will applaud with united voices, and, I fear, as unanimously disregard in practice. Our social gatherings are apt to be too formal, too expensive, too large to secure the end which we have in view. To give a "great party" once or twice a year, and astonish the whole community by the splendor of the show, is rather a poor way to cultivate genuine friendship. It is often a fearful undertaking to those who give it, and not very satisfactory to those who attend. Long and anxious debate settles on the list of the invited; and when it is too late to remedy errors, it is discovered that somebody has been forgotten. The worry about the invitations, the arrangements, and the weather, is a fearful tax upon the time and temper for weeks beforehand; and when the eventful evening comes the fear that all will not "pass off smoothly" keeps the host, and especially the hostess, in a tremor of excitement, which culminates with the assembling of the company, and finds relief in their departure. Of the multitude who move uneasily from room to room, it often happens that the majority are little more than mere acquaintances of the entertainers, and of each other. Some are invited because we know them well, and love their society; others, because they gave an entertainment some time ago, and an invitation in return for theirs is a sort of debt of honor, even when we suspect that their courtesy was only a little device whereby they were aiming to get into a new circle. Sometimes the invitations are extended so as to include some who are almost strangers, simply because a certain number must be reached, or the affair will be pronounced inferior to somebody else's party. There is no chance for genuine conversation; and little is heard save commonplace remarks about the crowd and the heat, or inquiries in regard to the old gentleman with the spectacles, or the young lady with the curls. Some fail to come, whose absence annoys and vexes; and others arrive first and stay last, whose absence could have been borne without a pang. Here is one whose sharp eyes and sharper tongue are the terror of the town, and who goes prying about, making mental notes of every small mishap, and every little awkward thing, and laying up ammunition for a gossiping campaign. There is another, who sees that his or her turn to give the entertainment is not far off, and who is carefully estimating the extent of the preparations to be made, and calculating the expenses to be incurred, in order to be equal to the rest, or, if ambitious, to outdo them.

I do not wish to visit these things with ridicule. They have some good features, as well as defects. They are worth something, perhaps, though not all that they cost. And yet there is "a more excellent way." If we invite at one time no larger a number than our parlors will seat, and we bring our friends together for a good, social, comfortable, leisurely talk, there might be less of display; but would there not be more of genuine enjoyment? Suppose, also, that the company be invited by families, including the young and the old, the parents and the children, the married and the unmarried. Let the grandsires draw their arm chairs toward each other and pour into each other's ear-trumpets the reminiscences of other days, and laugh again over the old oft-repeated stories. Let the little children, down on the floor by their side, discourse of tops or dolls, while middle age reasons on public events, or discusses family matters, and the young people are gathered around the piano or the book table; and as each drifts about on the social current, the spectacles and the curls impend over the same book or picture, and the ear-trumpet be found gathering up the voices that chatter over the toys. Thus there might be true social pleasure without anxiety or envy, without present uneasiness, or heart-burnings afterward. Thus the aged would be cheered by the vivacity of youth; and the gayety of youth be tempered by the wisdom of age.

Or, if any one fancies doing things on a

larger scale, let as many be invited as the house will hold comfortably; and instead of coming at midnight to stay till morning, let the company assemble early in the evening. And let there be music, and mirth, and laughter, and leisurely comfortable interchange of ideas, discourse that carries no sting and leaves no wound, but fosters gentle manners and lasting friendships. If the host chooses thus to manifest his hospitality, let there be a repast as good as need be; but excluding all that can intoxicate. Moreover, before the guests separate, let a few moments be spent in praise and prayer, according to the pious example of our fathers. And let midnight see all the guests safe at home. Thus the morrow will not find them jaded in body and mind, and irritable in temper, but clear in brain and warm in heart, with a tendency to smile all day long over the pleasant recollections of an evening thus innocently spent.

I own that I am not sanguine in regard to

the popularity of my proposed reform, especially in fashionable quarters. Young men who in the language of the day are called "fast," will pronounce this way of giving a party decidedly "slow." Mrs. Fitzshoddy sees that this mode of procedure will materially lessen her chances to display her newly acquired splendors, and thus totally extinguish her aristocratic neighbor over the way, who failed to return her call five years ago. Fitzshoddy himself has serious misgivings. He looks up at the social heights he would fain ascend, and shakes his head despondingly. "That is not the way them fellows does things, and you won't get among them unless you do as they do. They have a crowd, and a big fiddle, and a dance, and a long table with a wheelbarrow load of silver and things on it, and lots of wine, and all that. You can 't invite them to a hum-drum tea-drinking that winds up with psalm-singing and prayer. They would think it was somebody's funeral."

Miss Arabella, too, who has of late given her whole mind to the devising of gear for the outside of her head—a cunning piece of strategy to divert attention from the state of things within—dreads so much conversation. "People get to talking of things that you never heard of, you know, and books that you never read, and it is so embarrassing, you know." And then she absolutely trembles when she thinks of "Pa's" bad grammar, and his habit of shaking the windows with gigantic laughter at his own jokes. Many, too, will admit the evils of present social customs, but be afraid to lead in innovations. Some will feel that to refuse to give a grand party, after having attended a number among their acquaintances, will look very much like repudiation. Still, I doubt not that the intelligent and the conscientious will agree that what I have proposed is, as it has been already styled, "the more excellent way." I know that it will be hard to make the giddy believe that there is much enjoyment to be found in these quiet ways. They want a crowd, and noise, and commotion. And in this they judge amiss. This crazy rush after excitement defeats itself. As simple food and regular habits best promote health, so simple pleasures best promote genuine happiness. The joys of wine are not to be compared with the calm peace and self-mastery which belong to the temperate. The whirl of the dizzy dance, the wild excitement of the race-course, the sensational tricks of the theater, the whole circle of vices and fashionable follies are poor in their results, compared with the better pleasures which arise from our nobler nature. They who would enjoy life wisely and well, must not heed every voice which cries "Lo, here," or "Lo, there," but remember that "the kingdom is within."

CHAPTER X.

APPEAL TO THE YOUNG MEMBERS OF THE METHODIST EPISCOPAL CHURCH.

"*I have written unto you, young men, because ye are strong, and the word of God abideth in you, and ye have overcome the wicked one.*" 1 John ii, 14.

BEFORE we part, will our young Christian reader "suffer the word of exhortation?" I am not unmindful of the situation in which you are placed. You have associates, intelligent, agreeable in manners, and not immoral, who argue stoutly in defense of their thoughtless pleasures. Your conscience resists, and yet you feel the effect of their solicitations. You are sometimes almost ready to wish that your parents, your pastor, your class-leader, and your own conscience would consent to your yielding, that you might escape the pressure and feel no conflict between duty and the wishes of your gay companions. Let me call your attention to certain considerations, which I trust will have the effect to strengthen you for the right.

1. *Frivolous and doubtful amusements have always been condemned by the Discipline of our Church.*

Our General Rules do not indeed name dancing, the theater, and the rest. Had they done this, it might have been argued that the Discipline allows every folly not specified in the list. Our fathers in the Church were too wise thus to attempt to war against an evil which assumes a thousand Protean forms. They announce a broad principle, which condemns all "*such diversions as can not be used in the name of the Lord Jesus.*" Do you profess to be in doubt as to the true intent and meaning of the Rule? If you do, look at the past history of the Church. Which of the founders of Methodism favored dancing? Did John Wesley? Did Fletcher or Clarke? Which of them favored the theater or the horse-race? Did Hedding, or Fisk, or Olin? I challenge the apologists for dancing, theaters, and races to show that a single one of the multitude of holy men and women who have a name in our annals ever practiced or approved such diversions. On the contrary, there arise from their honored graves a great cloud of witnesses against them. The devoted servants of God, who shine as stars in our firmament, and whose names are "as ointment poured forth," condemned, feared, abhorred them as utterly at war with the life which they were living and the work which they were doing. Nor were these the views of ignorant, morose, narrow-minded people, soured by disappointment, or disabled by age or disease, but of intelligent, happy men and women, who served the Lord with glad hearts and went about with smiling faces.

Our Church traditions are unanimous in regard to these things. The testimony which they bear is uniform and strong. Our Bishops and pastors are now unanimous in their judgment. Within the past year, Conference after Conference has spoken in resolutions and pastoral addresses, warning our young people on this subject. If, therefore, a young man here and there among us finds that the practices into which he has fallen are at variance with the deliberate judgment of the Wesleys, the Clarkes, the Asburys, and the Heddings of the past, and all the Bishops and pastors of the present day, I respectfully suggest that he will not be liable to be convicted of excessive modesty if he should begin to suspect that his ideas on the subject are wrong, nor of excessive caution if he should conclude to refrain from indulgence till he is better assured that it is right and safe. Surely no one will count it a light thing to disregard the teachings of a century of spiritual power and progress, nor to turn a careless ear to the kind and faithful counsels of those who now watch for souls.

2. *Every member of the Methodist Episcopal Church is bound by a solemn pledge to abstain from all questionable diversions, such as those already named.*

In the form given in the Ritual for the reception of persons into the Church after probation, the fourth question is in the following words:

"Will you be cheerfully governed by the Rules of the Methodist Episcopal Church, hold sacred the ordinances of God, and endeavor, as much as in you lies, to promote the welfare of your brethren and the advancement of the Redeemer's kingdom?"

To this question, so full of meaning, each candidate for reception must answer, before God and his Church, "I WILL." (Discipline, page 156.)

Every member of the Church, therefore,

solemnly promises before God and the people of God to be cheerfully governed by the Rules of the Church. One of these Rules calls upon you to avoid "such diversions as can not be used in the name of the Lord Jesus." That Rule has always been understood to condemn balls and dancing, theaters, attendance at horse-races, and the whole list of corrupting amusements. The logical chain, then, is complete. Every member of the Church is bound, in the most solemn manner, by his or her own pledge, fully and publicly given, to abstain from balls, dancing, theater-going, and the rest.

Can you, for one moment, harbor the thought of repudiating so solemn an obligation? The Psalmist inquires, "*Lord, who shall abide in thy tabernacle? Who shall dwell in thy holy hill?*" And he thus answers his own question: "*He that sweareth to his own hurt, and changeth not.*" God honors those who are faithful to their word.

He delights in the man who keeps his promise, even when it is against his own temporal interests to abide by it. If God counts it a dishonorable and wrong thing for a man to repudiate a pledge given to his fellow-man, what will he think of those who repudiate a solemn public pledge made to him? If God honors the integrity of the man who keeps his word when his interests seem to call upon him to violate it, what will he say of those who violate their word when all their interests, both temporal and eternal, call upon them to keep it?

3. *When the young people connected with the Church are drawn into frivolous diversions, it is a sorrow of heart to the pastor and to all devoted Christians.*

Will it be replied that these faithful friends of years are so narrow and antiquated in their notions, that no one need care what they think or how they feel? The matter can not be disposed of thus lightly. It is not a small thing for a few young men and women, before whom real life lies yet untried, to set up their opinions, and blindly adhere to them, in opposition to the solemn judgment of the whole body of the ministry. It is not a small thing to wound, deeply and wantonly, those whose acknowledged consistency and holy lives are the joy and crown of the Church, and one of the main elements of its strength in the community. It is by these, and such as they, and God working through them, that we have Bibles and Sabbaths, and law and order, and civilization itself—all that exalts a Christian country above a heathen land. These devoted followers of Christ love his Church and his people. Some of them have been long in the way. They feel that they are approaching the gates of *the city which hath foundations*, and they are expecting daily the shadowy messenger that shall bid them enter. Looking to the younger members of the Church to supply the places which they will soon leave vacant, they may well be troubled, and shed their tears over the gloomy future, when they see youthful professors of religion given to vain and trifling pleasures and friv olous pursuits, trying to break down the discipline of the Church, and strip Methodism of its beauty and its power, and wrest from its hands the spiritual weapons with which a thousand victories have been won.

4. *When young Church members become giddy and fond of worldly pleasure, the unconverted are encouraged to go on in their sins.*

They who are yet unsaved hear the ways of wisdom described as ways of pleasantness and peace, but they know not how to understand the declaration. They confess that it is good to have a hope of eternal life, just as it is good to have a life-preserver about you when you are going to make a sea-voyage. Still, to them piety is a mystery. The deep joy of devotion, the glow and the rapture of praise, the blessedness of communion with God they can not comprehend. They listen, and wonder, and sometimes doubt and do not know what to think. But when they find that young members of the Church are just as eager as themselves after questionable pleasures, they conclude that these roseate pictures of the happiness of the Christian are, to say the least, overdone. When they see the flock trying the fence on all sides of the fold, and stretching their heads through every opening, to nibble at the weeds outside, they begin to suspect that the pasture within is not as rich as it is represented. Thus the inconsistent conduct of professed Christians who plunge into worldly amusements harms souls and injures a holy cause.

And sinners, too, are inconsistent with themselves. Now they argue that religion is all delusion, because, as they say, its professors are no better than other people; now they insist that their soulless pursuits must be right, because even members of the Church indulge in them. Thus they seek to justify their follies and their sins by the example of worldly Church members. Moreover, they will endeavor to make a little in you justify a great deal in them. Tell a sinner that he is not wise in attending balls, and he will twit you with the parlor dancing at some well-known professor's house. Warn him against the theater, and he will ask you to point out the moral difference between that and the play at the museum. Tell him that the gambling den is a dangerous place for young men, and he will remark, with a significant look, that living away from home he can not play cards in his father's house, as some do. And what professors of religion do occasionally, the unconverted, on the strength of their example, will claim the right to do constantly and habitually. Thus the thoughtless conduct of Church members is made to increase the perils which environ the unsaved, and to hedge up the only way of life. To incur, or even risk, consequences like these for the sake of a momentary excitement, is certainly to do the devil's work for low wages.

5. *If you indulge in diversions which are thus under condemnation, it can not fail to lessen your religious enjoyment and mar your usefulness.*

You may seem to yourself to be confident that your course is right, but the consciousness that others, whose judgment you must respect, believe it to be wrong, brings a cloud over you. The fact that you are doing what they condemn will haunt you in church, at the prayer-meeting, and every-where. The fact that you do this, not under any plea of necessity, but for mere pastime and momentary pleasure, will not mend matters. However kind and considerate the older members of the Church may be in their allusions to your course, you feel that you have not their confidence fully. This will trouble you, perhaps irritate you. You fancy that you are looked upon coldly. You detect little instances of neglect. You imagine that certain expressions in the sermons of your pastor or the prayers of your brethren were meant for you. Things get worse the longer you brood over them. You are tempted first to stay away from the sacrament, and then to neglect the other means of grace. Some well-meaning but clumsy brother pounces upon you at a most untimely moment, administers a scathing rebuke, and goes on his way happy, blessing the Lord that there is one Christian left who has the courage to do his duty. Now you are really angry. You are ready to imagine that all the rest of the Church would talk the same way if they should speak their minds. Thus, little by little, you veer from your Christian course, the mists gather around you, the stars disappear, you fall into adverse currents, and, it may be, finally strike upon the rocks, and make shipwreck of faith and a good conscience.

Will you say that the evils depicted flow not from your conduct, but from the censoriousness of the Church? If all were silent, the result would not be materially different. The Methodist Episcopal Church is immovable in her position in regard to these things. If you violate her Discipline, you can not shut out the thought that you are an unfaithful, disloyal member of her communion. This alone will suffice to bring a chill and a blight upon you. The world, too, see that you are not in accord with your brethren—not at home in the place which you occupy—and this encourages them to ply their arts to lead you still further. If you resist, they remind you of your own past conduct, and inquire, perhaps with a sneer, whence comes this sudden tenderness of conscience. If others rebuke them, they refer to you, with another sneer, as their exemplars. Surely, the poor pleasure which springs from questionable diversions is bought at too high a price when it costs us our consistency, the warm fellowship of Christian people, peace of conscience, and the power to do good.

6. *In morals compromises are not only treason to truth and righteousness, but compromised positions are of all the hardest to defend in argument and maintain in practice.*

You have acquaintances, intelligent and agreeable, but gay and inconsiderate, who are unwearied in their efforts to draw you into their circle. Their importunities are urgent, and it taxes all your powers of resistance to withstand them. You grow weary of the conflict between duty and inclination, and wish for rest. The thought occurs to you that if you go a little way with your tempters they will be satisfied, and no great harm will be done.

You reason amiss. To compromise with wrong is never the end of conflict. You must conquer a peace. If you do not mean to make a complete surrender to the world, the flesh, and the devil, there must be a point where the line is drawn, and the stand taken. Where will you place the line? Will you try to draw it half way between right and wrong? If you do you will abandon a strong position for a weak one. If you yield in regard to dancing in private parties, you will be invited, in due time, to attend a ball. If you go to see some "moral drama" performed at the museum, you will be urged to attend the theater. And the assault made on your half-way position will be just as strong, the conflict just as painful, and to refuse just as hard as you now find it. The place of undoubted right is at once the safest to occupy and the easiest to maintain, and it is bad generalship to try to intrench at any other point. And to parley with the enemy is the next thing to a surrender.

Fight it out, then, on this line. Life is

brief, and close beyond it lie heaven and hell. If you take one single step in the direction of danger and ruin in search of fleeting pleasures, will you think, ten thousand ages hence, that in this you were wise? The foolish diversions in which you are now importuned to join war with health, waste time, squander money, mar Christian reputation, dissipate serious thought, hinder usefulness, attack every temporal and every eternal interest. Can you persuade yourself that it is right for you, for the sake of an hour's feverish excitement, to tarnish your religious example, grieve your fellow-believers, lay a burden upon your pastor's heart, wantonly throw away your power to do good, and give new courage to the wicked?

Will you still try to apologize for questionable pleasures? The entire board of Bishops, the General Conference, your pastors, without an exception, all the deeply pious men and women of the Church, believe that dancing, card-playing, going to the theater and the races are unwise, inexpedient, hurtful to the spiritual interests of those who engage in them, and damaging to the moral power of the Church of God. Nor do they stand alone in this solemn judgment. The most intelligent and devoted Christians in the various Churches around us share these convictions. Will you set yourself in array against whole Conferences, Councils, and General Assemblies? And if you deem yourself equal in judgment to all combined, let me ask you another question: Is your conclusion as safe as theirs? They think it dangerous to dance, play cards, and attend the theater. Are you equally confident that it is dangerous *not* to dance, *not* to play cards, *not* to attend the theater? Is abstinence as perilous as indulgence? They fear that God will not hold you guiltless if you venture into these frivolities. Are you as fully persuaded that God will condemn you if you do not venture into them? The danger is all on one side. Beware how you venture where there is cause for hesitation. Remember, "he that doubteth," and yet goes on when he might safely stop, "is damned."

CHAPTER XI.

APPEAL TO THE CHURCH.

"*And they shall teach my people the difference between the holy and profane, and cause them to discern between the unclean and the clean.*" Ezekiel xliv, 23.

ON moral and religious questions compromise is treason to the right. Lafayette's witty and just illustration is well applied. He supposes two men to get into an altercation in regard to a fact in arithmetic. "Twice two is four," says the one, stoutly. "No," replies the other, "twice two is six." Both are immovable, and the dispute waxes warm. A third person approaches, and lays a hand gently upon each. "Gentlemen, reason is not infallible. The wisest men are sometimes in error. We are all prone to rush to extremes. You, my friend, affirm that twice two is four. You, who are equally my friend, affirm that twice two is six. Compromise, gentlemen, compromise. Meet each other half way. Agree to say, hereafter, that twice two is five."

Men are not lacking who, even in considering points of morals and religion, are ready to confess that really, after all, so far at least as their present information extends, twice two is somewhere about five. Nay, in their haste to meet what they style the demands of the age, some are ready to compromise at five and ninety-nine hundredths. And thus, all the way from what St. John calls "the camp of the saints and the beloved city" down to the place where Gog and Magog are gathering their hosts for battle, men are pitching their flimsy tents and raising their equivocal banners. It is a lamentable fact that among the chief obstacles to the progress of the Gospel we are compelled to count bodies that claim to belong to the Lord Jesus Christ, and yet have neither the heart to preach his doctrines nor the courage to proclaim his law. In all ages there have been sects of nominal Christians, who form a part of the Church of Christ in the same sense that the outside scales of a shell-bark hickory are a part of the tree, and who are ever ready to compromise with the world and tolerate all fashionable follies. Worldly men would manage the affairs of a Church in the same manner that they would conduct a political campaign. The argument is, that in order to be popular, and grow rapidly in numbers and in wealth, the Church must lay as few restrictions as possible upon candidates for admission, and as seldom as possible come into collision with the pleasures and the passions of the multitude.

Mr. Bright, in a recent speech in the British Parliament on the disestablishment of the Irish Church, gives, in a sentence or two, a correct description of this policy which we have here mentioned:

"The Right Honorable gentleman, the mem ber from Bucks, argued very much in favor of the Established Church on the ground that there ought to be some place into which people can get who would not readily be admitted any where else. The fact is, what the Right Honorable gentleman wants is this: that we shall have an established Church which has no discipline, and that any one who will live up to what may be called a gentlemanly conformity to it may pass through the world as a very satisfactory sort of Christian."

But the wisdom of this world is foolishness with God. This mercenary policy fails by the very measures to which it resorts. When the wicked see no distinction between the Church and the world they cease to respect the Church. Even the hypocrite finds his occupation gone when a profession of religion means nothing, just as the counterfeiter stops work when the bank fails and its notes are no longer current. Thus the cunning of men overleaps itself. On the other hand, the Church that boldly joins issue with sin wins moral power with every blow, and secures the respect even of the enemy. Thus they who feebly seek to save their lives lose them, while those who are ready to lose life for Christ's sake and the Gospel's find it.

The principle stated is of infinite importance, and we must neither forget it nor distrust it for an hour. All who fear God will confess that we are not to withhold the truth nor compromise with sin, even if the multitude desert our altars to crowd where the cross is lighter or its offense has wholly ceased. But is it true that worldly craft and policy will fail even as a policy? Let another question answer this. Other things being equal among rival denominations, have not the purest in doctrine and the strictest in morals always been the most successful?

Churches grow weak by lowering the standard of morals. When there is no discoverable difference between the Church and the world, the Church is no longer loved, or venerated, or believed. It becomes powerless to pull down the strongholds of sin; it can no more stir the heart, nor rouse the conscience, nor reach the mysterious depths of our nature; it ceases to meet the religious wants of those whose hearts God has touched, and men turn away unsatisfied from its shallow waters. The scorner will be loud in his denunciations of religionists whose vows are but the breath of the moment, and whose professions mean nothing. Even the soul convinced of guilt and danger will be afraid to trust to the guidance of a Church which has in it so little of the divine, so little of the power of God.

Methodism took at the beginning, and has held to this day, what some might regard as extreme positions on the subject of slavery, worldly amusements, and the drinking customs of the times. What is the verdict of history? Have we damaged ourselves by our fidelity to the right? Some timid, half-convicted people have doubtless been repelled from our communion by the strictness of Methodist discipline and the boldness with which we have assaulted the wrong, but who believes that the Church would have grown more rapidly by compromise and cowardice? Who believes that it would be wise, even according to the wisdom of this world, to compromise with evil now? Zion is not "lengthening her cords and strengthening her stakes" in a Scriptural manner when she "stretches the curtains of her tent" to shelter dancing, card-playing, and wine-bibbing converts. If these should come in crowds, offering on these conditions to join us, we could not receive them. To do so would be to act as madly as would the general who, in an enemy's country, commands his soldiers to throw away their arms, call in the sentinels, and level the intrenchments, in order to gain a few timid recruits who would not wear the uniform an hour if they thought that it meant war.

Nor is our argument disproved by the history of modern ecclesiastical organizations which have been less rigid than our own Church. In an intelligent community, where the Bible is read, their laxity is always against them. And in those very denominations the really pious, whose influence and example are the very salt of the body, to preserve it from putrefaction, and without whom it would hardly be recognized as a religious body at all, do not join in these questionable practices themselves, nor do they advocate them in others.

The way in which the world reasons about a facile Church is well illustrated by a conversation which actually took place not long ago between a sort of a minister and a shrewd, irreligious rich man, whom he wished to get in his little fold.

"Mr. B——," said the clergyman, "almost all your family have joined the Church, and I think it is about time for you to do the same."

"O, I am not fit to join the Church. I am not at all pious, you know," was the reply.

"But," said the minister, "you are aware that we are not very strict. Our Church does not require as much as some others."

"But I am not right," said Mr. B——. "I sometimes get angry and swear, and that will not do for a member of the Church."

"O, well," answered the minister, "you do not mean any harm by it, do you? That need not hinder."

"But, parson, that is not all. I am in business. I trade horses, for instance, and make the best bargain I can; and some people say that I tell lies in making my bargains."

"O, well," said the parson, "it is right for

us to take care of our interests. That need not hinder you."

"Now, look here, parson," said our friend, somewhat excited, "what good will it do me to join your Church if I need not be any thing but what I am? I am not a Christian now, I know; but if I ever join the Church, I mean to be one."

Even the world, unsaved, dim in vision, and hard in heart, has learned enough of the truth to despise those who are ready to sacrifice religion for the sake of numbers, and the pecuniary and social strength which numbers bring. If the Methodist Episcopal Church should abandon her traditions, and retreat from her present high position in morals, her apostasy would be attended by a fearful loss of religious power. If such an exhortation were allowable, I would call on all upon whom devolves the oversight of the Church to stand firm for the strict morals of Methodism. There is always a difficulty in maintaining Scriptural discipline. To enforce it is often painful to the pastor. It sometimes disturbs the membership and the community, interrupting friendly intercourse and exciting evil passions; nevertheless, we can not give up Church order. The pressure can be escaped only by a complete abandonment of discipline. Concessions and compromises merely transfer the battle to another point, where we must again fight, our forces demoralized by defeat and the enemy emboldened by victory.

If there is any place which we can hold against the enemy, any line where we can muster our forces and repel invasion, it is on the frontier. The king who fails to meet his foes the moment they set foot within his territory is already conquered. Drawing the line, and taking her stand in favor of total abstinence from all that intoxicates, the Methodist Episcopal Church has kept herself pure from the sin and shame of intemperance, and yet not one in ten thousand of her members is ever arraigned for violation of the stringent rule. Could the Church tolerate what is called "moderate drinking" without being compelled to deal with multitudes whom moderate drinking had led into the depths of drunkenness? For the same reason it is easier to keep our young people from objectionable diversions than to discipline them for the grosser inconsistencies into which indulgence would speedily lead them.

Will it be said that if we are so rigid our young people will leave us and join other communions? Be it so, if it must. They who are in haste to sell their membership in the Church for so poor and small a mess of pottage can do us little good if they remain. *They go out from us because they are not of us.* A thousand dancing, wine-bibbing, card-playing, theater-going Church members will not furnish one worthy candidate for the

Christian ministry, not one devoted class-leader, not one pious man or woman ready for the spiritual work of the Church of God. If they leave us in order to seek a more congenial home, we can better afford to lose than to keep them. The rubbing out of minus quantities increases the sum total. And if any other Church, so called, imagine that they can make their swarm the stronger by hiving our drones, they are certainly welcome to try the experiment. If there be a noble emulation that may justly prompt us to "labor more abundantly" than others, and excel them if we may, in Gospel successes, we need not fear the rivalry of any fashionable, worldly, easy-going denomination. Such as these will never "take our crown." Pure doctrine, a faithful ministry, unwavering adherence to the Divine law of morals, a devoted, holy, earnest laity, alone will win the prize.

But let us not flatter ourselves with the idea of a vantage-ground which no one else has the wisdom to see nor the grace to occupy. No low degree of morality will suffice to place us at the head of the sacramental host, or even give us a position among the leaders. Others as well as ourselves see the beauty of holiness, and are striving to put on the robe "white and clean" which is "the righteousness of saints." Almost every branch of the Church of Christ has taken the alarm, and, by its leading ministers or resolutions passed in ecclesiastical councils, has spoken emphatic words of warning. It would be easy to fill scores of pages with these utterances, coming from Churches differing widely in doctrine and in usage. A few extracts, with the sources whence they emanate, will show us the sentiments and convictions of the general Church in our whole land.

The General Assembly of the Presbyterian Church thus spoke half a century ago:

"On the fashionable though, as we believe,

dangerous amusements of theatrical exhibitions and dancing, we deem it necessary to make a few observations. The theater we have always considered as a school of immorality. . . With respect to dancing, we think it necessary to observe that however plausible it may appear to some, it is perhaps not the less dangerous on account of that plausibility. . . Let it once be introduced and it is difficult to give it limits. It steals away precious time, dissipates religious impressions, and hardens the heart."

The General Assembly of 1865 reaffirmed the action of the session of 1818, condemned card-playing—to which attention had been called by a memorial—and "affectionately exhorted all the members of the Church" to avoid "all recreations and amusements which are calculated to impair spirituality, lessen Christian influence, or bring discredit upon them in their profession as members of a Christian Church."

Bishop M'Ilvaine, of the Protestant Episcopal Church, thus declares his judgment on the same subject:

"Let me now turn to two objects, in which there is no difficulty of discrimination—the theater and the dance. The only line I would draw in regard to these is that of entire exclusion. And yet, my brethren, I am well aware how easy it is for the imagination to array both of these in such an abstract and elementary simplicity, so divested of all that gives them their universal character and relish, that no harm could be detected in either. And the same precisely can be easily done with the card-table and horse-race."

Bishop Mead, also of the Protestant Episcopal Church, thus condemns dancing:

"As an amusement, seeing that it is a perversion of an ancient religious exercise, and has ever been discouraged by the sober-minded and pious of all nations, on account of its evil tendencies and accompaniments, we ought conscientiously to inquire whether its great liability to abuse, and its many acknowledged abuses, should not make us frown upon it *in all its forms.* I will briefly allude to some of the objections to it. When taught to the young at an early age, it is attended with an expense of time and money which might be far better employed. It promotes the love of dress and pleasure, to which the young are already too prone; it tempts to vanity and love of display; it induces a strong desire to enter on the amusements of the world at an early period, in order to exhibit the accomplishments thus acquired, and to enjoy a pleasure for which a taste has been formed; it leads the young ones exactly into an opposite direction to that pointed out in the Word of God."

In their Episcopal Address of 1867, the Bishops of the Methodist Episcopal Church South thus speak:

"This is no time to abate our testimony

against worldliness in all its forms. Our Church has never faltered in its teaching or modified its tone in relation to dancing, theaters, the manufacture and sale of ardent spirits, drunkenness, revelings, and such like, as demoralizing and fatal to godliness. Now that we are threatened with these evils coming in like a flood, we renew our warning."

In 1866 the Young Men's Christian Association held a General Convention in Albany, New York. Delegates were present from all parts of the United States and the British Provinces. The question of amusements was carefully considered, and the conclusion reached was set forth in a formal resolution, thus:

"That we bear our energetic testimony against dancing, card and billiard-playing, as so distinctively worldly in their associations, and unspiritual in their influences, as to be utterly inconsistent with our profession as the disciples of Christ."

And last of all, but not least in the wisdom of the sentiments uttered, nor in the faithfulness of its warnings, we cite the Pastoral Letter of the Provincial Council of Baltimore, the voice of the Bishops of the Roman Catholic Church. It is dated May, 1869:

"The dangerous amusements, prominent among the evils we have to deplore, and which is an evidence of the growing licentiousness of the times, may be reckoned a morbid taste for indecent publications, and the frequency of immoral or positively obscene theatrical performances. No entertainments seem sufficient to satisfy the fast degenerating spirit of the age unless they be highly sensational, and calculated to gratify the most prurient appetites. We can hardly say who deserve a stronger condemnation, the actors who pander to the most vitiated tastes, or the audiences who encourage, by their presence, and applaud these grossly indelicate exhibitions. Both actors and spectators appear to vie with each in their rapid march down the slippery path of sin. We deem it particularly our solemn duty to renew our warning against the modern fashionable dances, commonly called 'German,' or round dances, which are becoming more and more the occasions of sin. These practices are so much the more dangerous as most persons seem to look upon them as harmless, and indulge in them without any apparent remorse of conscience. But Divine revelation, the wisdom of antiquity, the light of reason and of experience, all concur in proclaiming that this kind of entertainments can not be indulged in by any virtuous persons, unless they be more than human, without detriment to their souls, or even be present to take part in such amusements, where the eye is dazzled by an array of fascinating objects, where the senses are captivated by enchanting music, and the heart is swayed to and fro amid the surrounding gayety and excitement."

With these facts, arguments, appeals, and testimonies we leave the subject to the solemn consideration of the reader, believing that the position which we have taken is rational, Scriptural, and safe, "by manifestation of the truth commending" itself "to every man's conscience in the sight of God."

"FINALLY, BRETHREN, WHATSOEVER THINGS ARE TRUE, WHATSOEVER THINGS ARE HONEST, WHATSOEVER THINGS ARE JUST, WHATSOEVER THINGS ARE PURE, WHATSOEVER THINGS ARE LOVELY, WHATSOEVER THINGS ARE OF GOOD REPORT; IF THERE BE ANY VIRTUE AND IF THERE BE ANY PRAISE, THINK ON THESE THINGS."

www.ingramcontent.com/pod-product-compliance
Lightning Source LLC
LaVergne TN
LVHW011212110826
845150LV00006B/1408

9781425517359